T0274082

Dante and the
Night Journey

Dante and the Night Journey

ALAN WILLIAMSON

 FIRST HILL BOOKS

FIRST HILL BOOKS
An imprint of Wimbledon Publishing Company
www.anthempress.com

This edition first published in UK and USA 2023
by FIRST HILL BOOKS
75–76 Blackfriars Road, London SE1 8HA, UK
or PO Box 9779, London SW19 7ZG, UK
and
244 Madison Ave #116, New York, NY 10016, USA

British Library Cataloguing-in-Publication Data
A catalogue record for this book is available from the British Library.

Library of Congress Control Number: 2023932661
A catalog record for this book has been requested.

ISBN-13: 978-1-83998-744-1 (Pbk)
ISBN-10: 1-83998-744-8 (Pbk)

Cover Credit: Blake Dante Inverno II from Wikimedia commons

This title is also available as an e-book.

For Peter Dale Scott,

remembering our Dante conversations at the Durant Hotel

CONTENTS

PREFACE

ONE OF THE BEGINNINGS OF THIS BOOK—THERE WERE MANY—CAME WHEN I WAS TEACHING A SHORT CLASS ON THE INFERNO TO A GROUP OF YOUNG POETS AND FICTION WRITERS. They were an exceptionally astute, and mostly well-educated, group, but none of them had much background in Dante or the Middle Ages generally. We were discussing the wood of the suicides, where those who have taken their own lives are turned into trees. And someone started to notice similarities with the "dark wood" where Dante is lost in Canto I. Here is that famous beginning, in Robert Pinsky's translation:

> Midway on our life's journey, I found myself
> In dark woods, the right road lost. To tell
> About those woods is hard—so tangled and rough
>
> And savage that thinking of it now, I feel
> The old fear stirring: death is hardly more bitter.
>> (*Inferno*, p. 5. All subsequent citations are from
>> this translation, unless otherwise noted.)

As the "right road" is "lost" here, so the wood of the suicides is "unmarked by any path." And the word Dante uses for "lost," *smarrita*, recurs here to describe Dante's bewilderment. We went on to notice other verbal echoes: both woods are described as *aspra* (rough) and *selvaggia* (savage). And finally one of my students asked the obvious question: In his dark period, did Dante ever contemplate suicide?

An unanswerable question, of course, historically and biographically. Giuseppe Mazotta and Joseph Luzzi speculate that he did, in the grim period after he was exiled from Florence. But in general this is a kind of question professional Dante criticism, until recently, has rarely asked, even though it can be grounded, as my students' work shows, in the subtlest kind of close reading. For two generations now, it has been the fashion to read Dante and other medieval writers only in terms of the thought of their own time, especially its orthodox theology—Aquinas in Singleton's case, Augustine in Freccero's. This approach has produced remarkable insights, but it puts Dante very far away from us as twenty-first-century human beings. And it ignores the possibility that the *Divine Comedy*, like other masterworks, emits high frequencies that only later ages, informed by other experience, will be able to transcribe as conceptual thought.

But I have not written this book to argue with the professional Dante scholars, for which I entirely lack the competence. Therefore, there will be few footnotes and almost no scholarly apparatus. My intention, rather, is to restore the balance toward the human side of Dante, the personal and psychological story which many of us can identify with.

For another beginning of this book goes back many years. I began studying Dante when, "midway on our life's journey," I found myself in a dark wood. I had lost my first academic job and lived for years on short-term appointments, unable to publish my first book of poems. My marriage was shaky; my depression was deepened by harrowing obsessive ideas. My slow recovery seemed to me to parallel Dante's and even perhaps to be edged along by his. I came to feel, in short, that Dante's experience of Hell, and the return from it, however distant theologically, had something in common with my own.

Later I found out, anecdotally and through reading books like Luzzi's *In a Dark Wood*, that my experience with Dante was not unique. What the perplexed in spirit, like myself, find comforting in Dante is that he could have journeyed so far into the dark side of life, but was not trapped there: that he could escape to psychic health and even mystical vision. So I have written this book partly for people like myself who, however slight or deep their acquaintance with Dante, have been, in Robert Frost's words, "acquainted with the night."

But I'm also writing for those who teach Dante, whether to undergraduates or (as I did) to more advanced creative writing students. These students need a way to read Dante without having to master an arcane theological system, a way to connect him with their own twenty-first-century concerns. (Such connections can take odd forms: a friend teaching a group of nurses in an adult education program found them recognizing the diseases they had treated in the punishments of Inferno!) But most connections are more common. We all have problems coming to terms with sexual desire, anger and ambition—each the subject of one of the following chapters. Most of us have had to surmount periods of despair; many of us feel we are on a spiritual path, though increasingly often outside the framework of any religious denomination. If we learn to see Dante in this way, he offers not only wisdom but also companionship; he is a lens through whom we can view our own lives. He still has the power to show "the road to everyone, whatever our journey."

ACKNOWLEDGMENTS

I am grateful to Paul Breslin, Jeanne Foster, John Tarrant, and Richard Wertime, who read part or all of this book in manuscript, and made many useful suggestions. To Robert Pinsky, Brenda Deen Schildgen, and Peter Dale Scott, for many good conversations over the years, and for encouraging me to dare to think and write about Dante.

Excerpts from *The Inferno of Dante: A New Verse Translation* by Robert Pinsky. Translation copyright 1994 by Robert Pinsky. Reprinted by permission of Farrar, Straus and Giroux and Orion Publishing Group. All rights reserved.

Dante, excerpts from *Purgatorio*, translated by W. S. Merwin. Copyright 2000 by W. S. Merwin. Reprinted by permission of The Permissions Company, LLC on behalf of Copper Canyon Press, copercanyonpress.org, and the Wylie Agency.

I

THE NIGHT JOURNEY

IN *ARCHETYPES OF THE COLLECTIVE UNCONSCIOUS*, JUNG DESCRIBES THE
DREAM OF A THEOLOGIAN. It bears an extraordinary resemblance, as we
shall see, to Dante's situation in Inferno I:

> *He saw on a mountain a kind of Castle of the Grail. He went along a
> road that seemed to lead straight to the foot of the mountain and up it.
> But as he drew nearer he discovered to his great disappointment that a
> chasm separated him from the mountain, a deep, darksome gorge with
> underworldly water rushing along the bottom. A steep path led downwards
> and toilsomely climbed up again on the other side.*

Jung comments:

> The descent into the depths always seem to precede the ascent. [...] The
> dreamer, thirsting for the shining heights, had first to descend into
> the dark depths, and this proves to be the indispensable condition for
> climbing higher. (Jung, "Archetypes," pp. 302–3)

For Jung and his followers, this journey is an archetypal one, which
they call the "night journey" or "night sea journey." In mythology, and in
the early epic poems—think of Gilgamesh, Odysseus, Aeneas—it is literally a journey to the realm of the dead, as it is in Dante. So classical scholars call it by the Greek term *nekuia*.

But even in ancient times, such journeys are psychological as well as
eschatological. The "dark depths," for Jung, are the unconscious, of which
"[w]ater is the commonest symbol." In particular, they are the dark potentialities of the self, what Jungians call the "shadow." We might call it our

1

opposite, the place where we consign all the terrible possibilities we cannot stand to admit into our conscious image of ourselves. The infernal journey represents our need to come to terms with and assimilate it. And it is not something that only befalls gods and heroes. It can happen to any of us. So Joseph Campbell writes:

> The hero, whether god or goddess, man or woman, the figures in a myth or the dreamer of a dream, discovers and assimilates his opposite (his own unsuspected self) either by swallowing it or by being swallowed. One by one his resistances are broken. He must put aside his pride, his virtue, beauty, and life, and bow or submit to the absolutely intolerable. Then he finds that he and his opposite are not of differing species, but one flesh. (Campbell, p. 89)

The encounter, as ordinary people experience it, has much in common with what we call a "mid-life crisis." (Dante makes himself precisely thirty-five in the Divine Comedy—"midway on our life's journey," because according to the Bible, the human life-span is seventy years—"threescore and ten.") The crisis may come in the form of a life-altering event. So Robert Bly writes in *Iron John,*

> It is as if life itself somehow "discharges" him. There are many ways of being "discharged": a serious accident, the loss of a job, the breaking of a long-standing friendship, a divorce, a "breakdown," an illness. (Bly, p. 71.)

But, on a deeper level, the descent is necessary because we have not come to terms with our own inner problems, with the "absolutely intolerable." We have been naïve about the dark sides of ourselves, and of life. So our early successes—which may have been considerable—have lacked solid grounding. The painful and often, at first, seemingly futile struggles that follow as we try to reestablish our footing are the everyday equivalent for the monsters the mythic hero encounters on his journey: three-headed snarling Cerberus, Medusa whose stare can turn one to stone.

Bly has a wonderful metaphor for this stage in our progress. He calls it *katabasis*, or the "road of ashes." The fairy-tale prince or princess must scrape ashes in the kitchen, and learn that they are not exempt from common human fate. All forms of pride, from class-pride to, as Campbell puts it, "virtue, beauty, and life" must be ground to pieces before renewal becomes possible.

What was the nature of Dante's own plunge into the "road of ashes"? We have some indications, suggestive if incomplete. The early death of Beatrice Portinari (whom he loved from a distance, and to whom he addressed all his love poems, even though both were married to other people) affected him strongly. By some accounts, he became sexually profligate after her death. According to others, he immersed himself in the study of philosophy, becoming less interested in—if not altogether losing—his Christian faith.

Then there was his involvement in the tortuous maze of Florentine politics. As a prior, he had to consent to the exile of his best friend, the poet Guido Cavalcanti. Guido contracted malaria in exile, and died soon after his return to Florence. Dante will hint at his guilt over this in Inferno X.

But the defining tragedy of Dante's life occurred after the date when the Divine Comedy putatively occurs, but before the time of its writing. While Dante was on a diplomatic mission to Pope Boniface, the party opposed to his took control of Florence—with Boniface's connivance, Dante became certain. Dante and others of his party were exiled, in his case on pain of being burned at the stake if he returned. From then on, he would be dependent on the hospitality of various patrons to whom he was a cultural ornament or politically useful. The following is his account of that experience, in my translation, which I will be using for all citations from *Paradiso*, except when otherwise noted:

> You will learn how salty is the taste
>   Of another man's bread, and what a stony path
>   Leads daily up and down another's staircase.
>
> (Paradiso XVII, ll. 58–60)

As late as Paradiso XXV, he still hopes for his interdiction to be rescinded; it never was.

Whatever Dante's personal "road of ashes," the psychic and spiritual predicament of being lost in the dark night has never been rendered as powerfully as in the opening lines of Inferno. There are many fine translations of this passage, my favorites being Robert Pinsky's and Seamus

Heaney's. But I am going to offer my own literal, word-for-word one, drawing on Sinclair's prose rendering.

> In the middle of the journey of our life
> I came to myself in a dark wood,
> Because the straight way had been lost.

I love "I came to myself" and the passive voice in the third line. We do not know how we got into this state; it suddenly surrounds us. And we do not perceive ourselves as having any agency in the matter. Indeed, our sense of self is already too attenuated to encompass agency; that is what losing the way means. Later, Dante powerfully conveys the half-consciousness of this state, even while acknowledging some responsibility:

> I do not know well how to say how I entered there,
> I was so full of sleep at that moment
> when I abandoned the true way.

Trying to describe what the state of psychic darkness is like is, as all depressives know, almost impossible. Even if there is a particular symptom or obsession one can own up to, if one overcomes one's sense of shame, one cannot convey to others the emotional state that made that symptom so compelling.

> Ah to tell what it was is so hard a thing,
> that wood savage and sharp [or harsh] and fierce,
> the very thought of it renews my fear.

Finally, the state can only be defined in terms of itself, as Dante conveys in a wonderful Latin/Italian pun: *selva selvaggia*. The Latin word *silva*, "wood," is the root of the words for "savage" in all Romance languages. "Savage" things are things that happen in the woods. Seamus Heaney's translation is the most successful in trying to find an English equivalent: "in the thick of thickets."

I've wandered off the trail into the woods, during one of my visits to Tuscany. I wouldn't do it again. Even when the trees are sparse and the light gets through, the understory is almost impenetrable. Something "sharp" or "harsh," a bramble, the blunt, eye-level twig of some smaller bush, seems to spring up at every step. You doubt that you will ever break free. Dante's metaphor, as so often, is nothing but the fact. As Ezra Pound said, but Dante already knew, "the natural object is always the adequate symbol."

"The very thought of it renews my fear." The effort to describe the state is not only well-nigh impossible; it is also frightening. As Freud remarked, once a track is laid down in the brain, it is there forever. One's triumph is never complete; to describe or recall the state is always to risk falling back into it.

"So bitter it is that death is hardly more so," Dante concludes. But then he goes on,

> But to tell of the good I found there,
> I will tell of the other things I encountered.

Words that will resound like a bell for anyone who has come out on the other side!—whether to undertake a great project, to feel worthily loved by another person or simply to intuit a more integrated self one can stand to confront in the mirror.

We will, of course, respond to Dante's metaphors in the light of our own experiences with the dark side of life. I tend to see in them the shame, and inability to communicate, of obsession and depression. A friend whose difficulties have been more with impulsive and self-destructive acting-out finds in the sleepwalking state a powerful metaphor for denial—our inability to understand our own motives, our blindness to certain basic facts about our lives and where they are leading us.[1]

Dante, at the moment we have reached in the poem, is very far from attaining the "good" he speaks of. He has only just glimpsed its possibility, emerging from the dark wood. Like Jung's theologian, he looks up at a distant hilltop. And he sees that it is already lit by the sunrise, though everywhere below is still dark. (This is something I too have experienced, in a Tuscan valley in early spring.)

---

1 Thank you, for this and much else, to Richard Wertime.

5

> I looked up and saw its shoulders
> already clothed in the rays of that planet
> that leads men straight on every road.

There is so much magic in these three lines. The "shoulders" of the hill are an image both for the strength Dante does not yet possess, and for the fatherly figure who might carry him in the meantime. There is such poignancy in the admission that the sunlight is so readily available that its guidance is almost automatic for other people—but not for him. (And for us, though not for Dante's original readers, the multiplicity of "roads" suggests that Christian belief may not be the only path that can lead to spiritual renewal.) Even the medieval error of considering the sun a "planet" adds, for us, a certain wistfulness: there may be orders, authorities, even beyond what for us is the first force of life.

> And so the fear was quieted a little
> which had persisted in the heart's lake
> all that night I had passed so piteously.

> And as one who with laboring breath
> has escaped from the deep to the shore
> turns to gaze at the perilous waters,

> so my mind, which was still fleeing away,
> turned back to look again at the pass
> that never let anyone escape alive.

As untamed woods are a symbol, among other things, for the unconscious, so are bodies of water, in both Freudian and Jungian psychology. To be in the dark wood is to be immersed in one's inner underworld, unable to separate out the rational conscious ego. The "heart's lake," in medieval physiology, was a cavity within the heart where the emotions, particularly fear, resided. But when this lake is almost alchemically transformed into literal "perilous waters," from which a swimmer has barely escaped, there is no doubt of the psychological meaning. As in Jung, the waters are a portion of the psyche; what Dante has almost drowned in is his own mind.

How typical of those who have just glimpsed the sunlight at the same time to feel that their "fear" is "quieted," and to believe that their escape, even though it has just happened, is impossible! Still, the propitious "hour of the day" and the "sweet season" of spring give rise to a project in Dante's mind: like Jung's theologian, he wants to climb the hill directly, and reach the sunlight.

And now comes the episode which one of my students said should be required reading in all rehab facilities. For Dante's will is simply not strong enough to get him up to the top unaided. Three beasts assail him—a lion, a leopard and a she-wolf. Criticism has, from the beginning, been almost unanimous in interpreting these as destructive forces in the psyche as well as in the world: the leopard lust, the lion pride or anger, the she-wolf greed or insatiable craving. And they drive Dante back down. Like the rehab patient, he simply does not have enough control over his own impulses to become the person he would like to be. Dante's failure to ascend by the direct route is almost as terrible to him as his initial despair. As Pinsky's translation has it, he "was ruining [him]self back down."

Joseph Campbell's account of the night journey story provides us with a good framework for understanding what follows. At the moment when the task the hero has been called to seems impossible, Campbell says, a guide or guides will appear. They are often two in number—one male and one female. They will not only get the hero into the underworld; they will help him overcome its terrors, its dark gods who will test him or deprive him of some of the powers he could summon up on his own. They will be there at the times the traveler is so paralyzed with the horror of what he has seen—Medusa's face—that he fears he will stay there paralyzed forever.

Dante's two guides are the poet Virgil and his first love, Beatrice. For Beatrice has come from heaven, out of fear for Dante's spiritual predicament, and called Virgil out of Limbo, where he dwells with the other virtuous pagans, to lead Dante through hell and purgatory. Virgil appears at the very moment of Dante's greatest discouragement and tells him that in order to ascend he must first descend. He must go among "the lost people": metaphorically, he must confront and acknowledge the worst places his own unintegrated instincts might lead him, the worst possibilities in human nature and in his own. Only then can he escape from hell into the suffering of purgatory, which is potentially redemptive.

But why Virgil? The early allegorical commentators agreed that, as a virtuous pagan, he stands for Reason, and what it can achieve without the help of Grace. Reason can show us the difference between right and wrong, and why some wrong actions are worse than others. It may even lead us to self-government and a truly free will, but not to a vision of the divine. (It helped, for this use of Virgil in a Christian poem, that the Middle Ages believed Virgil had prophesied the coming of Christ.)

But it's important that Virgil is a poet, indeed Dante's favorite poet. And he is the poet who wrote of a descent into the underworld, in the Aeneid Book VI. There was no model for handling such subjects in the vernacular literature of Dante's time, limited as it was to love poetry and chivalric romances. That is why Virgil's voice "seemed weak from long silence." He is Dante's guide, partly but importantly, because he will teach Dante how to write such a poem, the very poem we are reading.

If Virgil is Dante's first guide, Beatrice, who has sent him, will take over from him at the summit of purgatory, to guide Dante through Paradise. But the reunion with Beatrice at the summit of purgatory, in the Earthly Paradise, plays an extraordinary double role in the story, according to Joseph Cambell's schema. The heroes who have passed through what Campbell calls the "road of trials," who have integrated the "absolutely intolerable" into their sense of self, are prepared for far more than simply the accomplishment of their original goals. Their further extraordinary progress involves three stages. The first, Campbell says, is a "mystical marriage […] with the Queen Goddess of the World." Then there is an "atonement with the father," and finally "Apotheosis," an equivalent to Buddhist Enlightenment or the Christian Beatific Vision, in which the voyager sees God in himself and himself in God. And the adventure does not end even here. The hero is requested, as the Buddha was by the supreme god Brahma, to return to ordinary life in order to share the transcendent wisdom with humanity.

We will have occasion to talk about "atonement with the father" and "Apotheosis" later in this book. But surely his reunion with Beatrice in what was the Garden of Eden is Campbell's "mystical marriage." And this despite the fact that it is nonsexual, and indeed begins with a scolding. But it is what makes Dante's ascent to, and understanding of, Paradise possible.

Dante's night journey story is extraordinary, in comparison to earlier ones, in a way that we haven't dwelt on yet. The protagonists of earlier epic poems are heroic figures central to the founding stories of their cultures: Gilgamesh, Odysseus, Achilles, Aeneas, Beowulf. Here, for the first time in literary history, a long poem tells the story of an ordinary human being, Dante Alighieri of Florence, the son of a prosperous family, just below the level of the nobility. We learn of his involvements in Florentine politics, the unhealing wound of his lifelong exile from his native city, and his hatred of its instigator, as he believed, Pope Boniface. (He manages to get his revenge by putting Boniface in hell when, at the putative time of the poem, Boniface was still alive.) Dante's friends, his mentors, his fellow poets and his enemies people the three realms of the afterlife, along with contemporaries whose stories he knew only through gossip. And, as we have seen, it is his actual first love who greets him at the summit of purgatory, becoming his symbol for divine grace.

It is indeed a breakthrough in literature's ability to take our ordinary humanity seriously. Since Dante, there have been many night journey stories whose protagonists are not huge figures on the mythic or historical stage. To take just three examples, from twentieth-century literature: Joyce's Stephen Dedalus leaves Dublin for Paris with premature expectations of immediate artistic greatness. He falls into his "ashes" when he must come home to a paltry teaching job and nights of heavy drinking. On a hallucinatory visit to "Nighttown," Dublin's brothel district—but also, obviously, the "Night" side of the psyche--he is rescued by an unlikely father figure, Leopold Bloom. Dedalus' recovery is not detailed, but since he is semiautobiographical, the very existence of Joyce's book *Ulysses* testifies to it.

And Tayo, the Laguna Indian protagonist of Leslie Marmon Silko's *Ceremony*, returns from World War II with a war psychosis in which the world has turned to "smoke." Neither Western medicine nor traditional native healers can cure him. Then he encounters an unorthodox healer and, later, a lover who appears to be the incarnation of a goddess. With their help, he accomplishes a dangerous task important to his family and, symbolically, to the whole future of his people.

Or, turning to poetry, we might look at Adrienne Rich's great poem "Diving into the Wreck." It follows the version of the story called the night sea journey, the paradigm being Jonah's descent into the belly of the whale.

Arming herself with the accoutrements of Jacques Cousteau's equipment, the speaker descends to the sea floor. Entering on the journey brings both feelings of "blacking out" and of "power," but ultimately a different kind of consciousness is called for.

> the sea is another story
> the sea is not a question of power
> I have to learn alone
> to turn my body without force
> in the deep element. (Rich, pp. 22–4)

What is found on the sea floor will yield "treasures," but it is, in every sense of the word, a "wreck." It is the disaster we carry with us from our own personal histories as well as from the history of the world, in particular, for Rich, of its gendered relationships. To understand it, we must recover our own intimate experience of it, not rely on received interpretations, because in ourselves "we are the half-destroyed instruments / that once held to a course." "[T]he book of myths" may be part of our initial equipment, but ultimately what we need is "the wreck and not the story of the wreck."

The context of Rich's parable is profoundly feminist, yet the identity forged in it goes beyond gender: "I am she: I am he." And it applies to everyone: "We are, I am, you are." Her quest for intimate, not received, knowledge of the "damage" and her belief that however particular to one life, it is also universal resonate with Dante's own.

In the night journey, we inevitably wrestle with some of our deepest human impulses. As in a successful therapy, our accommodation with them is transformed; we are more in control of them, and less likely to let their more destructive potentials take control of us. And with that transformation our projects are also altered—or equally valuably, we are given a new permission to go ahead with them.

Let's look back, now, at the three beasts that drive Dante back down. The leopard, we remember, stands for lust; the lion must stand for, or at least include, anger; the she-wolf is more variously interpreted but includes, as Pinsky translates it, "all the world's cravings"—all our desires that our life be different from what it is. These are, then, the most challenging areas in our quest for spiritual or psychic progress; so I shall devote a chapter to each of them. Taking this approach, I will be following each topic through the entire Divine Comedy, not progressing in an orderly manner through the three realms of the afterlife. The fifth chapter will look at how Dante's account of the Antepurgatory parallels many of our own experiences of "the tremulousness of recovery." Finally, we will see how *Paradiso* dramatizes a change in the sense of identity from the personal to the universal. It also presents us with extraordinary modes of consciousness, which anticipate not only psychoanalytic ideas but one of the strangest case histories in contemporary neuroscience.

▮▮

LOVE

NO ISSUE IS MORE CENTRAL TO OUR INDIVIDUATION THAN HOW WE DEAL WITH SEXUAL DESIRE AND ITS PROBLEMATIC CONNECTION TO OUR DEEPEST WISHES TO KNOW, AND BE KNOWN BY, ANOTHER HUMAN BEING. First, there is the matter of controlling our instinctual impulses, rather than being controlled by them; or, in other cases, to overcome neurotic inhibition without doing avoidable harm to other people and to oneself. But then, there is the involvement of erotic need with our need to be recognized, to be seen as we truly are—a subject we will explore more thoroughly in Paradiso. As we shall see there, that need may be even more fundamental than sex itself, since it reaches back to the most profound happiness and disappointment of infancy, the presence or absence of the "mirroring" mother. We may hope all these needs may be reconciled in monogamous marriage. But real-life marriages require a great deal of honesty and hard work to lead to mutual growth, rather than mutual confinement.

There are, in short, no ready-made solutions. So Rainer Maria Rilke speaks, in *Letters to a Young Poet*, of "the many conventions that have been put up in great numbers like public shelters on this most dangerous road." Marriage, of course, is one of those conventions. But so are the immoral arrangements such as prostitution and kept mistresses. They are "cheap, safe, and sure, as public amusements are" (Rilke, pp. 72–3).

Joyce's Stephen Dedalus, whom we've spoken of before, began in profligacy, going to prostitutes before he was fifteen. But he then reverted to the most ascetic kind of Catholicism, until he had a glimpse of a girl at the seashore, "an angel of mortal youth and beauty." He does not approach her, but she returns his gaze, so there is a kind of recognition. She suggests to him that the sacred and the sensual can be reconciled, that his true vocation is to be an artist, not a Catholic priest. But one could argue that

Joyce's own individuation was not complete until he could imagine the inner life of an actual woman, in the last chapter of *Ulysses*. (The putative date of the action of that novel is June 16, 1904—the day on which Joyce met the barmaid who would become his lifelong companion.)

Dante too struggles with these issues throughout the Divine Comedy. Though he is best known for his idealizing love of Beatrice, there is evidence that he went through a period of sexual indulgence during his years of depression, if not throughout his life. The poet William Butler Yeats intriguingly suggested, in "Ego Dominus Tuus," that what Dante created in the Divine Comedy was a sort of anti-self, the very opposite of his personality as a flawed human being:

> Being mocked by Guido for his lecherous life,
> Derided and deriding, driven out
> To climb that stair and eat that bitter bread,
> He found the unpersuadable justice, he found
> The most exalted lady loved by a man (Yeats, p. 158)

But Dante's situation must also be considered within the cultural context of medieval Europe. There, among the upper classes, marriages were almost always arranged, a matter of familial and political alliances. Dante's wife belonged to a family a little above his own in the Florentine hierarchy, the Donati. But she did not follow him into exile, and her existence remains unacknowledged either in the *Divine Comedy* or in its autobiographical predecessor, the *Vita Nuova*.

Instead, Dante's literary account of romantic love is focused entirely on Beatrice, whom he fell in love with at first sight when he was nine years old. Beatrice remained a somewhat peripheral but always earth-shattering presence in Dante's life. When he ran into her unexpectedly at a party, he fainted. When she didn't return his greeting in the street, having heard rumors of some misbehavior on his part, he was thrown into a tortured striving for self-improvement. And when she died young, he fell, as we have seen, into profound depression and perhaps sexual promiscuity. But he also made a vow to write of Beatrice "what has never been written of any woman" (Dante, *Vita Nuova*, p. 153). *The Divine Comedy* was the result.

This history may seem odd indeed to modern readers. But it followed a preexisting model in Dante's time, a tradition intimately involved with the birth of great lyric poetry in the vernacular Romance languages: Courtly Love. In this tradition, the lover, usually also a wandering poet, or *troubadour*, fell in love from a distance with an unattainable woman. It might be someone he had glimpsed once in church; it might be an Oriental princess he had only read about. More often, however, it was the wife of the nobleman who was his patron. Such loves were expected to be unconsummated; at most, a kiss was allowed after twenty years. If they were consummated, the results could be disastrous. Ezra Pound, in his *Cantos*, tells the story of a nobleman who discovered his wife's affair with a troubadour named Cabestan. He had Cabestan killed, cut out his heart and served it to his wife in a stew. When the wife was told what she had eaten, she declared she would never eat anything more, and threw herself out the castle window.

The unrequited, or long postponed, love was of course the occasion for an endless fountain of poetry. But it was also regarded as a moral education for the lover. He strove to make himself perfect, in order to be worthy of the idealized beloved. His devotion to her might even lead to a religious vision of the highest Good that she represents. The idea is not new in the Middle Ages; it is often called the Platonic ladder, because it goes back to Plato's *Phaedrus*, in the context of Greek homoerotic love between an older man and an adolescent. But it acquired a peculiar force in Dante's Florence, where the group of young poets among Dante's circle, Guido Cavalcanti and the poets of the *dolce stil nuovo*, were so devoted to it that they seemed almost a secret society, or a private religion. And, of course, their work was to give a decisive shape to the whole development of Western lyric poetry. A generation after came Petrarch, with his lifelong Platonic love for Laura. And in our own tradition, the Renaissance English sonnet began with translations from Petrarch.

The scenario of Courtly Love will seem quaint, even perverse, to modern readers, especially after the explosion of sexual freedom in the 1960s. But some scholars have suggested that it was part of a huge rediscovery of the feminine in Western culture, after the puritanical misogyny of early Christianity. The worship of the Virgin Mary in the Catholic Church and the huge cathedrals built in her honor stem from the same period and the same country, France, as troubadour poetry and Courtly Love. And in the Jewish tradition, across the Pyrenees, the figure of *shekinah*, God's female counterpart in the Kabalah, makes her appearance at around the same time.

Be that as it may, the church took a dim view of Courtly Love. However Platonic it was in theory, the cultivation of erotic sentiments in art might be an inducement to adultery and fornication. And, even while it was constructing cathedrals to the Blessed Virgin, the church found the elevation of any mortal woman into a kind of savior—as Dante does, more even than any of his predecessors—dangerously close to idolatry.

Dante first has to confront the dangers of sexual love in Inferno V, where the souls of the lustful are blown around in an endless circular wind. It's not a terrible punishment as punishments in the Inferno go; indeed, the circle of the lustful is the first circle (and therefore the least bad) that Dante enters after he leaves the Limbo of virtuous pagans and unbaptized infants. Dante follows Aristotle and Aquinas in regarding sins of incontinence, the over-indulgence in impulses not evil in themselves, as far less culpable than sins involving violence or malice. He is not one of our modern puritans for whom "sin" and "sex" are synonymous. And even in Inferno V, there are distinctions. The merely lustful are compared to starlings. The great lovers of antiquity and chivalric romance are cranes. And two, as we shall see, are faithful doves.

I've long felt an intuitive connection with this punishment, because of something a friend said about a failed relationship of my own. It was very intense, and ended my first marriage, but it lasted only a year. My friend said, "it had no place to land." She meant, I think, that we had plunged into it knowing little of the differences in each other's habits and values, the dailiness of our lives. But something larger seemed implied.

The center of Inferno V is Dante's encounter with Francesca—one of the most justly celebrated character portraits in the entire Commedia. Francesca, tricked into marriage to the deformed Gianciotto Malatesta, fell in love with her husband's brother Paolo. When Gianciotto discovered them together, he killed them both (the sin that will destine him for Caina, the circle of Hell for those who betray their kindred).

Francesca is one of the few characters in the Inferno—Farinata and Ser Brunetto are others—who seem to maintain a sense of personal worth quite independent of their damnation. Witness her first words to Dante, asserting the independence of her wishes from those of "heaven's king," in the interest of courtesy, gratitude and generosity:

> If heaven's king bore affection
> For such as we are, suffering in this wind,

Then we would pray to Him to grant you peace
For pitying us in this, our evil end.

(Inferno V, ll. 81–4)

Francesca goes on to describe her love for Paolo in terms that expressly echo the love poetry of Dante and his predecessors:

Love, which in gentle hearts is quickly born,
Seized him for my fair body—which, in a fierce

Manner that still torments my soul, was torn
  Untimely away from me. Love, which absolves
    None who are loved from loving, made my heart burn
With joy so strong that as you see it cleaves
  Still to him, here. Love gave us both one death.
    Caina awaits the one who took our lives.

(Inferno V, ll. 88–96)

The first line, as has often been noted, echoes both Guido Guinizelli's most famous poem, "The gentle heart betakes itself always to love" (*Al cor gentil ripara sempre amore*) and a poem of Dante's own, "Love and the gentle heart are but one thing" (*Amore e'l cor gentil sono una cosa*).

Here I must ask the reader's indulgence if I digress, briefly, on the very different responses to Francesca in the relatively conservative, historicist criticism of the twentieth century, and in earlier criticism. For the great nineteenth-century critic Francesco de Sanctis, Francesca inspired nothing but admiration, affection and pity. She was "the first real flesh-and-blood woman to appear on the poetical horizon of modern times." Beatrice, by contrast, is not "a character but a type or a category, not a woman but the Womanly, the Eternal Feminine of Goethe." She has never held readers' affections in the way that Francesca has. Francesca has "no vulgar or wicked qualities like hatred, rancor, spite […] she has no room in her soul for any feeling but love." Her prayer for Dante, knowing that it cannot reach God, is "one of the finest, most delicate and gentlest of sentiments, realistically portrayed." De Sanctis makes the same point about her appreciation of Dante's empathy; responding to his wish to know her story, she uses the word *affetto*, "affection," not "desire" or "curiosity" (De Sanctis, pp. 33–52).

Renato Poggioli's famous essay "Paolo and Francesca," by contrast, exemplifies the moral conservatism that often accompanies historicist approaches in the twentieth century (Poggioli, pp. 61–77). His argument, based on close comparison of historical texts, is subtler than I can summarize here. But Poggioli finds Francesca haughty and aristocratic. For him, her use of the word "gentle" (*gentil*), despite the echoes of Guinizelli's and Dante's sonnets, where it refer to inward kindness and sensitivity, means primarily "nobly born"—"gentility of blood." Her diction, far from being the model of sincerity de Sanctis saw, is "fashionable" and "conventional"—the conventions being those of the love romances by which she has been corrupted. And Poggioli maintains that if "That day we read / No further" refers to lovemaking, as seems obvious, it would be the utterance of "a harlot, devoid of the last shred not only of modesty, but even of self-respect." (For de Sanctis, her indirection here is a further indication of "modesty and chastity of feeling.")

Poggioli's essay particularly focuses on the deleterious effects of courtly love literature, the possibility that life imitates art. It was, of course, an issue that already troubled Dante, because of the church's disapproval. The core passage comes when Dante cannot help being curious as to "how and in what shape / Or manner did Love first show you those desires / So hemmed by doubt?" The answer is famous, even notorious:

> One day, for pleasure,
> We read of Lancelot, by love constrained:
> Alone, suspecting nothing, at our leisure.
>
> Sometimes at what we read, our glances joined,
> Looking from the book each to the other's eyes,
> And then the color in our faces drained.
>
> But one particular moment alone it was
> Defeated us: *the longed-for smile,* it said,
> *Was kissed by that most noble lover*: at this,

This one, who now will never leave my side,
   Kissed my mouth, trembling. A Galeotto, that book!
   And so was he who wrote it; that day we read

No further.

(Inferno V, ll. 112–24)

Galleotto, the go-between for Lancelot and Guinevere, was a medieval synonym for "pander." Is Dante too a pander, since his love poetry is echoed in Francesca's self-justification? When Dante faints dead away at the end of the Canto, many critics have suggested it is not just from overwhelming pity but from a sense of guilt and complicity.

And so, Poggioli says, Francesca cites the conventions of love literature in order to justify her "adultery" by clinging to "the idealizing and sublimating illusions which literature creates around the realities of sex and lust." It's perhaps no accident that this statement so closely resembles T. S. Eliot's statement, in his book on Dante, "that the love of man and woman," without the "higher love […] is simply the coupling of animals" (Eliot, p. 65). I've sometimes wondered—though this is, of course, purely speculative—whether the moral conservatism in so much historicist criticism can be traced, in part, to Eliot's prestige and influence. He was a great poet, but a sexually tormented man. His early poems displayed a marked sex nausea. He took a vow of celibacy while he was still married. His lifelong devotion to Dante helped to make the Divine Comedy required reading for all aspiring poets, but his personal problems may also have contributed to the narrow biases of historicist criticism.

But Eliot and Poggioli, and their contemporaries, are not alone in being worried by the possibility that life imitates art, with disastrous consequences. We find even the contemporary poet and Dante translator Robert Pinsky expressing mild skepticism, in his poem "The Night Game," at the fact that

Some of us believe
We would have conceived romantic
Love out of our own passions
With no precedents,
Without songs or poetry. […] (Pinsky, p. 86)

But I don't think we need to overemphasize either crude sexuality or the misleading power of literature, to understand what it is that Francesca fails to see when she attributes her predicament to a little quarrel with God. The point of Paolo and Francesca's punishment is finally this: that to ask another human being to fulfill one's entire need for comfort, absolute love, purpose in the universe, is to ask the impossible. The larger desire remains incompletely fulfilled, because only God, or the totality, could fulfill it. It keeps us, literally and figuratively, running in circles. This is the famous *contrapasso*—the method whereby the punishment is the sin itself, expressed in metaphorical terms. To whirl about in endless circular winds is not simply to re-experience the violence of passion. It is a metaphor for the endless search for something in a place where it cannot be found.

And this brings me back to think about my own experience. I had, I realized, asked way too much from my infatuation: I was looking to love to help me reinvent my sense of myself. ("I grew a face I could love," I wrote at the time.) Rilke, not surprisingly, had some wisdom on this subject, centuries after Dante. He sees the danger too much reliance on love can pose to the individual's own self-fulfillment. "Loving does not at first mean merging, surrendering, uniting with another person (for what would a union be of two people who are unclarified, unfinished, and still incoherent—?), it is a high inducement for the individual to ripen, to become something in himself, to become world in himself for the sake of another person" (Rilke, p. 69). The problem, in short, is not erotic love itself; it is the tendency to make love the all-defining goal in life, as so much in our culture encourages us to do.

To return to the question of art and love. Whatever its importance in Inferno V, Dante does intuit, as another German writer, Thomas Mann, would in our own time—and, indeed, as Plato did—that there is a connection between music and poetry and the unruly instincts, which resists our efforts toward a purely rational and ethical life. There is a relevant, even amusing, episode early in *Purgatorio*. Immediately after arriving on the island of Purgatory, Dante encounters Casella, a musician friend from his early life. He asks Casella to play one of the songs on which they have collaborated,

> to comfort
> with it my soul which, on the journey

20

here with its body, has become so weary.

(*Purgatorio* II, ll. 109–11)

Casella complies, singing his setting of a poem of Dante's closely akin to those that misled Francesca:

> *Love that speaks in my mind persuading me,*
> he began then, so sweetly that even now
> the sweetness goes on sounding in me.
>
> My master and I and the people who
> were with him seemed as content as though
> there was nothing else touching their minds.

(*Purgatorio* II, ll. 112–17)

Contentment, it would seem, even for the newly saved, even for Virgil himself, requires some appeasement of the instinctual life, some suspension of the life of the conscious, worrying mind. Later, the souls are compared to doves "quietly feeding / without their usual puffed-up displaying." But all is not well here, from the ethical point of view. Enter Cato, the stoic Roman whom Dante made the gatekeeper to Purgatory, even though he was a Pagan. Cato interrupts the proceedings mid-line and mid-sentence, "shouting, 'What is this, lingering spirits?'" From the ethical man's point of view, absorption in art is a "negligence," an interruption in the quest for self-perfection which should be unceasing. Still, as the whole tone of the passage conveys ("the sweetness goes on sounding in me"), Dante is more than half on Casella's side. When he compares the listeners to doves, he is of course reusing the metaphor applied to Paolo and Francesca in Inferno V. What is admirable in Francesca's "gentle heart" is not being repudiated, but carried along on the path to salvation.

Dante, in short, is not about to give up on either poetry or the ideal of love it celebrates. There are very few poets in Hell; Purgatory teems with them. There is the troubadour Sordello; there is the Roman poet Statius, for whom Dante invents a secret conversion to Christianity, to rescue him from Limbo. On the final terrace, where sins of lust are purged, Dante encounters two of his preeminent literary ancestors, and greets them with reverence: Guido Guinizelli, he of "The gentle heart always betakes itself

21

to love," and the troubadour Arnaut Daniel, to whom Dante pays the ultimate homage of allowing him to speak in his own language, Provencal.

Dante gets more definitive answers on the role of erotic love in an integrated life, and its relation to poetry, when he enters the Heaven of Venus, in Paradiso VIII and IX. The heavens below the level of the sun in Dante's medieval cosmology (those whose planets still are subject to change) are reserved for those whose devotion to God has been slightly compromised by some other dedication. (Though, as Dante makes clear, this demotion is only apparent; all the saved are equally in the presence of God.) The spirits in this "third heaven" move in an "eternal dance"—the opposite, but also the transmutation, of Francesca's perpetual motion.

And here we might pause to consider continuities of imagery through the *Commedia*, which can be obscured by too exclusive an attention to the *contrapasso*. We've seen how the images of the dark wood recur in the wood of the suicides. Now we might note how all the sins involving Eros display some version of perpetual motion: the circular winds of Canto V, the sodomites who can never stand still on the burning plain, the love poets in the ring of fire in Purgatory. Paradise does not dispense with this imagery. Instead, it completes what was previously incomplete, giving the motion the beauty, containment and satisfaction of dancing.

The souls in the Heaven of Venus are particularly marked by their generosity, their eagerness to encounter Dante and receive his questions:

> And ah, to see how its size and brightness flared,
>   Hearing my words, as if joy visibly grew
> On earlier joy!
>
> (Paradiso VIII, ll. 46–8)

No spirit there "rejoice[s] at the thought of doing someone a kindness" more than Cunizza. Dante is said to have known her when, as an old lady, she had taken refuge in Florence in the home of the Cavalcantis, the family of Dante's best friend Guido. In her youth she was notorious for her many love affairs and marriages, including an affair with the troubadour Sordello. In her old age, she was noted for her generosity; she freed the serfs who had belonged to her brother, a notorious tyrant whom we have encountered in Inferno.

The episode with Cunizza is one of Dante's great mini-portraits, summing up a whole personality in a few lines. It is easy to believe that he himself spent time with her, as an impressionable young man. Her generosity is shown first, as we have seen, in her eagerness to greet him. It shows again in the quickness with which she turns from speaking about herself to praising the spirit that stands beside her, as a "dear, radiant jewel." But in between comes a remarkable piece of self-assertion:

> I shine here because the beauty of this star
> Overcame me; for which I do not blame
>
> Myself unduly, and no longer care
>   To think about it—which seemed a little strong
>   To your Florentine gossips, when I lived there.
>
> <div align="right">(<i>Paradiso</i> IX, ll. 32–7)</div>

Cunizza's indifference to the gossips of Florence, and their preoccupation with sexual peccadillos, is like Shakespeare's in the Sonnets: "I am that I am, and they that level / At my abuses reckon up their own." But how can she "no longer care" about offenses that are punished severely in Inferno? The answer might be found in the similar words of her companion in the Heaven of Venus, Folco:

> Yet here we smile at such things—not at the fault
> Itself, which we have forgotten—but at the heavenly
>
> Power that ordained, and, foreseeing, by His art
>   Shaped it to so much good. […]
>
> <div align="right">(<i>Paradiso</i> IX, ll. 103–5)</div>

The same warmth, the readiness to connect with others, that made Cunizza amorous as a young woman has been transformed into the generosity Dante witnessed in her old age—and, indeed, that he encounters in all the souls in the Heaven of Venus. This is "the great result": sexual energy is not suppressed, but, in Freud's terms, sublimated, from an obsession with a particular erotic other to an active love of human beings in general, and of God.

Folco, the "dear, radiant jewel" beside Cunizza, will not be as sympathetic a figure to modern readers as he was to Dante. In his youth, he was a troubadour, and he says—almost boasts—that Dido, whom we've seen in the whirling winds of Inferno V, "could / Do no more folly" for erotic love than he did. But after he became a monk, and later a Bishop, he was one of the most bloodthirsty persecutors of the Albigensians, the "heretical" Manichaean sect that for a while threatened Catholic dominance in the south of France. Dante, unfortunately, was too much a man of his time to see Folco's career as a persecutor as a blemish. Rather, it indicates that Folco's sexual energy has been transformed into an equally fiery love of the church. (Though perhaps Dante does register some unease, as he so often does, between the lines, when he refers to an earlier time when the harbor of Folco's city, Marseilles, was "warm with its own blood" (*Paradiso* IX, l. 93). Folco's warmth, too, had bloody consequences.)

But it is Folco, I think, who resolves the question about the relation between art and love, in one extraordinary line:

> While I lived, I stood
> So strongly under the sign of this bright heaven,
> It bears some stamp of me.
>
> (*Paradiso* IX, ll. 94–6)

How can he have put his stamp on heaven itself? The only way I can read this is that love poetry adds something to the experience of love, even in heaven. Here the whole issue of life imitating art is at once raised and put paid to. The distinction between natural love and imaginary love matters terribly for the eternally frustrated seekers in Inferno V. But in Paradiso IX, it does not matter. Imagination and reality are both, after all, God's creation. St. Bonaventura, the Franciscan philosopher to whom Dante owed a great deal, wrote: "So great is the force of the highest good that nothing can be loved except through desire for it" (Saint Bonaventura, pp. 25–6). This is equally true of the physical attraction of one created body for another, and of the conception of Platonic love as a moral education. The difference between the souls in Heaven and those in Hell is quite simply that the former have understood this; the latter have not.

For Dante, of course, the great culmination of his own struggles with love is his reunion with Beatrice in the Earthly Paradise. As Joseph

Campbell would inform us, this follows an archetype in the Night Journey story; the hero's ordeals end in an encounter, even a sacred marriage, with the Great Goddess. We have seen this in some of our other points of reference. Stephen Dedalus's encounter with the girl on the beach is perhaps a sacred marriage; all of the female initiatrixes in Tayo's life are to some degree avatars of the Great Goddess.

Dante's ultimate ordeal, before his reunion with Beatrice, is to pass through the wall of fire where Arnaut and the other lustful souls suffer. Symbolically, this confirms that his attachment to Beatrice, however sublimated, is deeply erotic. He will again use of the fire metaphor when he sees her for the first time: "I recognize the signs of the old burning." But it also suggests that Dante must master the purely instinctual side of desire before he can achieve complete love.

The sacred marriage is in many ways an odd one. It begins, as we've noticed, with a scolding, Beatrice taking Dante particularly to task for the *pargolett[e]* (young girls) with whom he consoled himself after her death. But it is at the moment of scolding him that Beatrice calls him by his name ("which of necessity is here noted," Dante says, presumably because it breaks a medieval convention of artistic tact). Here we come, I think, to the relation of erotic love to the basic human need for recognition. And this recognition must come from an other who sees our worst sides, though also forgiving them. It is only when Dante is given his real name, in Beatrice's scolding, that he becomes his full self.

But another odd thing about this sacred marriage is that Dante is offered an alternative love object before he actually meets Beatrice. Dante has just begun to wander through the Earthly Paradise when he comes to a small but impassable stream. On the other side of it, "there appeared to me there

a lady all alone, who was singing
as she went, and choosing flowers among
the flowers with which all of her path was painted."

"Ah, fair lady who was warmed by the rays
of love, if I trust appearances,
which often bear witness to the heart,

may it be your pleasure to come closer
alongside this stream," I said to her,
"so that I can hear what you are singing.

You make me remember Proserpina,
where she was and what she was like, that time
her mother lost her, and she was the Spring."

(*Purgatorio* XXVIII, ll. 40–51)

The lady, who will later be called Matelda, complies with Dante's request, and then

she made me the gift of raising her eyes.

I do not believe that such a light shone
from under the eyelids of Venus when
her son's arrow pierced her, against all his custom.

(*Purgatorio* XXVIII, ll. 63–6)

This does, in a very real sense, go against the "custom" of the reader's expectations. For in any other context, it would be the beginning of an all-absorbing courtly love romance. What is going on? Is this a plot-complication, something that might interfere with Dante's reunion with Beatrice? Is there an allusion, perhaps, to some relationship in Dante's life far more meaningful than the *pargolette* Beatrice holds in such disdain?

The marvel is that there is no interference. Dante has already had a premonitory dream in which the two women appear as Leah and Rachel, the two wives of Jacob in the Bible—an allusion that makes clear which is the true beloved. But even more important, perhaps, is the injunction Dante has just received from Virgil, after he has passed through the seven terraces of Purgatory:

Your own will is whole, upright, and free,
and it would be wrong not to do as it bids you,

therefore I crown and miter you over yourself.

(*Purgatorio* XXVII, ll. 140–2)

He is even told, "From here on your own pleasure must guide you."
So Dante is now in control of, not subject to, his impulses, and even his "pleasure" is safe. He can recognize how beautiful and lovable a woman Matelda is and respond warmheartedly, without being for a moment deflected from his true goal, Beatrice. It is the equivalent of Cunizza's transformation of her own sexual impulses into general magnanimity. So one might think of the passage regarding the heavenly realm, earlier in Purgatorio:

> It [love] gives of itself according to the ardor
> it finds, so that as charity spreads farther
> the eternal good increases upon it,
>
> and the more souls there are who love, up there,
> the more there are to love well, and the more love
> they reflect to each other, as in a mirror.
>
> (*Purgatorio* XV, ll. 69–75)

Or one might think of a great love poem in English, John Donne's "The Good Morrow":

> For love all love of other sights controls,
> And makes one little room an everywhere.

As Dante and Beatrice ascend through Paradise, the imagery of fire continues, but it is more and superseded by a visual imagery of light. One of the basic premises of Paradiso is that Beatrice's beauty increases with each passage to a higher level. And as her beauty increases, so does Dante's confidence in her love for him. In Canto IV, he writes:

> Love, like sparks of the divine
> Itself, so filled her eyes, my powers failed me
>
> (*Paradiso* IV, ll. 139–41)

Poggioli, in the essay we have referred to, emphasizes the difference between the "smile" (*riso*) of Guinevere in the courtly romance and purely fleshly mouth (*bocca*) that Paolo kisses (Poggioli, pp. 62–3). The smile contains the essence of the personality, whereas the mouth is merely the object of carnal desire. So it is not surprising that, as we move higher in Paradise, Beatrice's smile becomes more and more her defining feature. In Canto VII, her smile is such that it "would make a man happy in the fire" (*Paradiso* VII, ll. 17–18). In Canto XXI, as they ascend to the Heaven of Saturn, she refuses to smile at him, because he would be incinerated, as Semele was when Zeus revealed himself in his full glory. But in Canto XXIII, she tells him that, because of what he has seen and learned, he has "gained strength to bear my smile" (*Paradiso* XXIII, ll. 47–8).

We can interpret all of this allegorically. Beatrice stands for divine grace, and her increasing beauty for the increasing brilliance of insight it brings, which the soul must grow in order to endure. But we can also see it as the splendor of the individual living being, as that being is perceived by its Creator. In his last description of Beatrice's smile—or rather, his confession of his inability to describe it—Dante writes,

> The beauty that I saw there so transcends
>   All we know here, that I truly believe
>   Only its Maker fully comprehends
>
> And joys in it.
>
> (Paradiso XXX, ll. 19–21)

Later in the passage, Dante writes, reusing the metaphor from Canto IV, that looking at her smile is like looking into the sun, and "deprives [his] mind of its very self" (*Paradiso* XXX, ll. 26–7). But this deprivation is not the dangerous loss of self Rilke warns us against; it is, as we shall see in the final chapter, the transcendence of the ego which is necessary for the Beatific Vision. Surely, whatever this moment represents allegorically, it is the great culmination of the love story. Ultimately, to fall in love is to approach the Creator's own vision of the splendor of His creation. To quote Bonaventura again, "so great is the force of the highest good that nothing can be loved except through desire for it."

ANGER

THERE IS NO DOUBT THAT DANTE WAS A VERY ANGRY MAN INDEED. Vindictive tirades fill the pages of Inferno, and extend even into Paradiso. Nearly every province or city-state in Italy is cursed at some point, or given some vividly demeaning description. His first biographer, Boccaccio, said that he would throw stones at a child or an old woman if they disagreed with his politics (though some Dante scholars question Boccaccio's veracity or good faith).

But consider the ingenuity with which Dante puts his archenemy, Pope Boniface, in Hell even though Boniface was still alive at the putative date of the poem. The stratagem goes like this. The simoniacs—those who sell pardons and the like, or use their ecclesiastical position for financial gain—are buried upside down in clefts in the infernal rock, with flames dancing on their feet. (This is a parody of the flames dancing on the Apostles' heads at Pentecost; the simoniacs have turned spiritual values upside down, putting the feet—material considerations—where the head should be.) A special cleft is reserved for the evil Popes; when a new one dies, his predecessor is pushed completely underground to make room for him. And so we have Dante approaching the flaming feet of Pope Nicholas III, who cannot see him, and who cries out

> "Boniface, are you already standing there—
> Already standing there?" The writing lied
>   By several years!
>
> (Inferno XIX, ll. 48–50)

Virgil says, "Answer him quickly: say you are not him, / Not who he thinks" (*Inferno* XIX, ll. 57–8). By the false recognition, Dante has managed to damn a living enemy!

The Middle Ages did not necessarily disapprove of anger and cruelty. Criminals were executed as cruelly as they were in the Roman Empire, and such executions were regarded as public entertainments. Heretics—those who broke with the established religious consensus—were burned at the stake, and sometimes tortured and mutilated beforehand. (Witness the horrific contemporary accounts of the deaths of Fra Dolcino and his mistress, which Dante predicts in Inferno XXVIII.) The punishments in Inferno, however ingeniously they function as allegories of the inner nature of the sin, are not that far removed from actual punishments Dante might have witnessed. In fact, as Dante notes, hired assassins were buried alive upside down, just as the simoniacs are.

So we might conclude, as many critics have, that Dante was simply a man of his time, for whom anger was neither a moral nor a psychological problem. Even some of the blessed spirits in Paradise get angry at what they see going on on earth. As we have seen, Dante puts Folco, one of the most bloodthirsty leaders of the Albigensian crusade, in the heaven of Venus. And when Dante rejoices at the torment of Filippo Argenti, in Inferno XIII, Virgil praises him: "Indignant soul, blessed indeed / Is she who bore you" (*Inferno* VIII, ll. 42–3).

It is certainly true that being justifiably indignant at real wrongs may be a necessary part of the spirit's growth. At the very least, it is an energizing escape from the passivity of despair. And it may serve some social good. But when we encounter anger among the seven deadly sins in Purgatory, Dante gives us a clear sense of how damaging, and how unpleasant, it is as a permanent state of mind. As Dante enters on the terrace where anger is purged,

> a smoke was
> coming toward us that was as dark as night,
> nor was there anywhere to escape from it

(Purgatorio XV, ll. 142–4)

He goes on to say,

> As a blind man goes along behind his guide
> so that he does not lose his way or hit
> something that could hurt or perhaps kill him,
>
> so I walked through the bitter and foul air

(Purgatorio XVI, ll. 1–13)

First, we notice, obviously enough, that the smoke is blinding. When anger takes over our minds, we believe our own narratives completely. We have no conception of how the situation might look to our supposed adversaries, or to an objective observer. We do not always know whether we are "hit[ting]" an enemy or a friend, and, if we are dealing with an enemy, we have no realistic idea of what power they might have to "hurt or perhaps kill" us.

But, beyond that, the smoke seems worse to Dante than the "murk of Hell" itself. It is "rasping" to all the senses, "nor was there anywhere to escape from it." I think anyone who has been consumed for a long time by anger or a grudge will recognize the force of Dante's metaphor. It is not the initial fire of indignation that is the problem, but the residue, the "smoke," it leaves in the mind. "Bitter" and "rasping," if it dominates it will eventually drive out all gentler or consolatory feelings. Dante is not only aware of the damage anger can do to others; he is aware of the equally terrible damage it does to one's own mind.

Of all the emotions, anger most immediately forces into contact with what Jungians call the "shadow," the worst potentialities within ourselves. So it's not surprising that nowhere else in the Inferno do we see Dante so clearly mirroring, in his own behavior, the sins he sees punished than in the episodes involving anger. This is even true of the scene with Filippo Argenti, notwithstanding Virgil's approval. Filippo is where he is because he was "furious," in life as in the afterlife; Dante becomes furious with him.

Dante's fury becomes actively violent in the final cantos of Inferno, in Cocytus, the hell of ice where sins of betrayal (whether of country, kindred, guests or benefactors) are punished. In Canto XXXII, stumbling among those half-buried in the ice,

> I don't know whether by will or fate or chance—
> Walking among the heads I struck my foot
> Hard in the face of one, with violence
>
> That set him weeping
>
> (*Inferno* XXXII, ll. 73–6)

Later in the same canto, there is no question of "will or fate or chance"; Dante deliberately tears the hair out of a spirit's head, to force him to disclose his identity.

With the ice, we pass beyond mere anger into the terrain of cruelty and atrocity. The ice is one of Dante's most universally resonant symbols. Whatever sins he intends for it to punish, it is the absolute zero of empathy, of the warmth of human connection that makes life, even at its worst, endurable. For contemporary readers, it inevitably calls up memories of the wars and atrocities of the twentieth century. The weather of Cocytus, in particular, takes our imaginations to the terrible winters of the European war: the Battle of Stalingrad, naked prisoners lined up on their way to the gas chambers at Auschwitz. To moments like the one Primo Levi records, when a death-camp guard breaks off the icicle from which a prisoner is licking precious drops of water. To Levi's baffled *Why?*, the guard responds, *Hier ist kein warum*. Here there is no why; here there don't have to be reasons.

The survivor's, and indeed the world's, response to that level of atrocity is inevitably complex. Grief is the usual way back to moral health, the way that keeps us open to empathy with all victims and fellow sufferers. But in mourning there is an element of acceptance; how does one accept the unacceptable? Retaliatory rage may seem the preferable, the more virile response, but rage can never end, since the crime can never be undone. It locks victim and persecutor, prosecutor and defendant, in a terrible and eternal twinship.

Nowhere in literature is that twinship so compellingly enacted as in the great episode of Ugolino. At the end of Canto XXXII,

> I saw two shades frozen in a single hole—
> Packed so close, one hooded the other one;

> The way the starving devour their bread, the one
>   Above had clenched the other with his teeth
>   Where the brain meets the nape.

> (*Inferno* XXXII, ll. 125–9)

The "one / Above," Ugolino had been imprisoned in a tower in Lucca by his enemy, Archbishop Ruggieri, who then had the tower door nailed shut, so that Ugolino and his children, imprisoned with him, starved to death. As many take it, Ugolino was driven by hunger to cannibalize his children's dead bodies. Now, throughout eternity, he repeats the crime on its perpetrator, satisfying his hunger with the Archbishop's brains.

Ugolino's story is so affecting that readers almost forget (as with Paolo and Francesca, or, later, with Ulysses) that he too is a sinner and deserves to be in Hell. Modern commentators, unwilling to base their interpretations on a technicality which has no emotional weight in the poem (Ugolino too is a traitor; he did betray the Pisans' castles), have argued that Ugolino's real sin lies in his response to his fate. Here, the core question is that of grief versus rage. As he tells his story, Ugolino asks Dante to grieve for him: "And if not now, when do you shed a tear?" But when he hears the tower door nailed shut, "Inside me I was turned to stone, so hard / I could not weep; the children wept" (*Inferno* XXXIII, ll. 38, 46–7). The next day, "I bit my hands for grief," and the children, thinking "I did it for my hunger's pain," say, "Father: our pain

> Will lessen if you eat us—you are the one
>
> 'Who clothed us in this wretched flesh: we plead
>   For you to be the one who strips it away.'
>   I calmed myself to grieve them less."
>
> (Inferno XXXIII, ll. 54–60)

Ugolino's "grief," which is really despair, with more than a hint of guilt, is too terrible to be shared with his fellow victims—lest it reveal to them their approaching fate. Instead, it becomes an inward-directed rage, as he bites his own hand. But the children's response is quite the opposite. For the critic John Freccero, it is Christlike, in its lack of self-preoccupation, its immediate and willing self-sacrifice. Ugolino, Freccero says, does not understand this; he

> seems to be unaware of the Christological significance of the children's suffering and his own. As they die, they echo the words first of Job—"The Lord gave, and the Lord hath taken away"—and then of the Saviour on the Cross—"My God, why hast thou forsaken me?" Ugolino's response is simply to repress his own grief for fear of increasing theirs.

The children's apparently naïve offer of their flesh echoes Jesus' offer to the disciples in John 6: "Whoso eateth my flesh[…] hath eternal life."[…]. Because Ugolino does not understand, there is no redemption. (*Inferno*, note, p. 424)

What Freccero does not say—but it seems clear enough—is that Dante the character follows the example of Ugolino, expressing grief only as rage. As the poet Peter Dale Scott, whose thinking in this area has influenced mine more than I can easily sort out, writes in *Minding the Darkness*, Dante

> when invited to weep
>
> at the fate of Ugolino
> > cursed Pisa and all its children
> > until the sight of Beatrice
>
> released from his frozen heart
> > a great deluge of tears

(Scott, pp. 217–18)

The curse is indeed one of startling ferocity:

> Ah Pisa! You shame the peoples of that fair land
> > Where si is spoken: slow as your neighbors are
> > To punish you, may Gorgona shift its ground,
>
> And Capraia, till those islands make a bar,
> > To dam the Arno, and drown your populace—
> > Every soul in you!

(*Inferno* XXXIII, ll. 76–81)

Dante justifies his curse on the grounds that "it was wrong in you to so torment / [Ugolino's] helpless children" (*Inferno* XXXIII, ll. 83–4). But, one might ask, are there not similar helpless innocents to be found among "every soul" in Pisa? Is not Dante perilously close to repeating the crime of Archbishop Ruggieri?

Some readers, I suppose, may still put Dante's curse in the same category of righteous indignation Virgil praised in the case of Filippo Argenti. But I believe the structure of Canto XXXIII, both narrative and symbolic, places the moral ambiguity of Dante's behavior at the center of attention.

For Canto XXXIII is an extraordinarily broken-backed piece of work, unless one presumes some subtler thematic governing principle. Where the other great set-pieces (Francesca, Ser Brunetto, Ulysses) all terminate with their respective cantos, Ugolino's story and the curse against Pisa bring us only to line 90. The rest of the canto tells a completely different story, bringing us round, however, to a precisely parallel curse against Genoa and all *its* inhabitants:

> Ah Genoese—to every accustomed good,
>> Strangers; with every corruption, amply crowned:
>> Why hasn't the world expunged you as it should?
>
> (*Inferno* XXXIII, ll. 148–50)

The climactic placement of the two curses, I think, forces us to consider Dante's propensity to damn the innocent along with the guilty as part of the ultimate moral coldness he is exploring in the hell of ice.

For, between the two curses, Dante commits his own greatest act of treachery, promising, and then refusing, to clear the ice away from Fra Alberigo's eyes. He justifies the act by asserting a complete reversal, or suspension, of moral norms: "to be rude / To such a one as him was courtesy" (*Inferno* XXXIII, ll. 146–7).

The equivocations surrounding Dante's broken promise are easy to catch and even chuckle over, but their ultimate moral meaning is harder to assess. "[I]f I don't help you then, / May I be sent to the bottom of the ice" (*Inferno* XXXIII, ll. 111–12). We know that he will go there—will have to haul himself up the tufts of hair on Satan's thighs—but only as a tourist. Or is it only as a tourist? "Oh souls so cruel that here, / Of all the stations you're assigned the last," Fra Alberigo addresses Dante and Virgil (*Inferno* XXXIII, ll. 104–5). It is a mistake that other damned souls have made before, but Dante's behavior, from the moment he enters the realm of ice, is "cruel," the cruelest we have seen from him in the poem.

Moreover, it is almost at the moment when Fra Alberigo addresses Dante, thus, that Dante first feels the "wind" from the "bottom" of Hell, the wind created by Satan's wings. But he hardly knows he feels it, because "as when a callus has grown numb, / The cold had sucked all feeling from my face" (*Inferno* XXXIII, ll. 95–7). It's hard not to conclude that the physical loss of feeling symbolizes a moral one; that Dante's incapacity for human sympathy, which reaches its culmination here, is the beginning of his encounter with the truly Satanic.

The ultimate argument of Canto XXXIII—its subtle, subterranean genius—lies in the continued manipulation of the theme of tears. The inability to weep, figurative or psychological in Ugolino, becomes literal in those more deeply damned:

> There, weeping keeps them from weeping—for as they do,
> Grief finds a barrier where the eyes would weep
> But forced back inward, adds to their agonies;
> A crystal visor of prior tears fills the cup
> Below the eyebrows with a knot of ice.
>
> (*Inferno* XXXIII, ll. 90–4)

The "prior tears," frozen over, force any new tears back as an "agon[izing]" pressure on the eyeball. Here, the tears that cannot be expressed are themselves the punishment; allegorically, their terrible constriction surely stands for the pain of isolation, and deadening of feeling, in the inner self. And these are the tears that Dante refuses to clear away from Fra Alberigo's face.

Now look back at the curse against Pisa: the Arno, the two islands that will block it at its source, sending its water back to drown all the Pisans. […] It is the same figure! A flow, a blockage and then the backward turning of the same flow as an endless malignity, against the self or against others. Dante's anger, concretized in Capraia and Gorgona, *is* the punishment he witnesses, and will not sympathize with, in Fra Alberigo.

And, of course, the two images repeat a third image, from earlier in the canto, the "nailing shut" [of] the door to Ugolino's "fearful tower." All three nailings-shut denote the final exclusion of someone—Ugolino and his children, Fra Alberigo, "every soul" in Pisa—from the bonds of human commonality. The finality of atrocity and the boundless repercussions of unbounded anger resonate in the figuration as in the story itself.

Dante invents one more terrible metaphor for this finality, in the strange fiction that makes up most of Fra Alberigo's story. "[A]s soon as a soul commits betrayal / The way I did," Fra Alberigo says, it "falls headlong" into Hell, and "a devil displaces it /And governs inside the body until its toll / Of years elapses" (*Inferno* XXXIII, ll. 124–8). What Dante means, I think, is that certain acts prevent the soul from changing, from giving its life a new significance, as even the worst of ordinary sinners can. To be sure, this serves Dante's need to put men like Fra Alberigo outside the moral pale. But my main reaction to this passage has always been horror and pity for the zombie-like body above that "eats and drinks and sleeps and puts on clothes" (*Inferno* XXXIII, l. 136), but has no further moral life. I have felt the same watching Claude Lanzmann's *Shoah*, listening to the hollowed-out voices of death-camp guards, telling their stories to a narrator who, like Dante, breaks promises, because he feels no bond of reciprocal humanity. *Hier ist kein warum* is turned back on its perpetrators.

Dante's passage through the "bottom of the ice" may be the most vivid image in literature or mythology for the night journey in Joseph Campbell's sense of incorporating the "intolerable." For the means of transportation is the body of Satan himself. Virgil, with Dante on his back, lowers himself down the devil's "shaggy flank [...] gripping [...] From tuft to tuft" (*Inferno* XXXIV, ll. 72–3). If the hairy imagery is not insalubrious enough, the center of the earth ("the place / All the other rocks converge and press their weight") is at "the pivot of the thighs, / Just where the haunch is at its thickest" (*Inferno* XXXII, l. 3; XXXIV, ll. 75–6). Critics have argued whether the center is the devil's anus, his penis or a point in between. Be that as it may, when Virgil has passed that point he turns himself around and starts to climb, still "grappl[ing] the hair" as his means of ascent. Dante does not understand "what point I had passed" when they emerge into "a kind of natural dungeon" (*Inferno* XXXIV, ll. 79, 89, 95). He is astonished to see Satan's legs looming above him, rather than his head.

One might emphasize, here, the narrowness of Dante's passage, when he has just confronted the worst sides of himself, and just before it begins to open out again. So C. G. Jung writes, "The shadow is a tight passage, a narrow door, whose painful constriction no one is spared who goes down to the deep well" (Jung, "Archetypes," 305). Though Jung has in mind "well" in the sense of water, it is no accident that it applies so accurately to Cocytus itself.

Dante's error, in not seeing what point he has passed, has a poignant meaning in terms of the story of recovery, which we will examine in Chapter V. When we reach the nadir of our night journey, our darkness of spirit is so complete ("I neither died not kept alive," Dante says—*Inferno* XXXIV, l. 28) that we cannot recognize a turning point, though we, and others, will in retrospect. And the first stages of our journey upward will still take place in grim and uncomforting circumstances, only "As far from Beelzebub as one can be / Within his tomb" (*Inferno* XXXIV, 129–30). One is never far from what has tormented one to begin with, for the whole first stage of our journey.

The cavity Dante and Virgil discover will ultimately lead them up "once more [to see] the stars." But at first it is "a place one cannot know by sight," but only by the "sound a little runnel / Makes" as it descends from the world above (Inferno XXXIV, ll. 140, 130–2). The sound is cheering, despite the darkness (in Italian, "runnel" is the mellifluous *ruscelletto*). Perhaps it stands for the intuition that precedes rational conviction, and that must guide the first steps of our upward journey.

But to return, in conclusion, to the theme of grief and anger. While I was first working on this chapter, I came on some musings by the late Michael Mazur, the great illustrator of Robert Pinsky's translation of Inferno:

> I think that the most overriding element of the whole *Inferno* is not
> the horror of the *Inferno*. It is, in fact, the sadness of the *Inferno* [...] .
> There is this strange rhythmic movement of water through the whole
> *Inferno* down to the ice field at the end. Sometimes it's blood; sometimes
> it's water; sometimes it's sewage. And in each case, it comes from one
> mysterious source, some old man who is shedding his tears in a faraway
> land, supposedly Crete. Those tears then turning into rivers and the rivers
> turn into large areas of ice. (Mazur, p. 37)

The old man of Crete appears in Canto XIV. Hidden inside Mount Ida, he is the mourner (and perhaps the former king) of the Golden Age, which the ancients located in Crete:

> Every part but the gold head bears a crack
>   A fissure dripping tears that collect and force
>   Their passage down the cavern from rock to rock

Into this valley's depth, where as a source
   They form the Acheron, Styx, and Phlegethon,
   Then their way down is by this narrow course

Until, where all descending has been done,
   They form Cocytus—and about that pool
   I will say nothing, for you will see it soon.

(Inferno XIV, ll. 94–102)

So the ice is itself frozen tears, like the tears that block Fra Alberigo's eyes. It is, finally, another metamorphosis of the Virgilian "tears of things."

In Peter Dale Scott's reading of the poem, Dante's tears when confronted with Beatrice's reproaches respond not only to her, but to every instance throughout the *Commedia* when he has repressed his grief. And indeed, at that very moment, Dante calls back the image of ice melting, which takes us directly back to the end of *Inferno*:

the ice that had been clamped around my breast
turned to breath and water, and came forth
out of my breast through the eyes and mouth.

(Purgatorio XXX, ll. 97–9)

It is as if Cocytus itself had finally thawed.

We live in a time when grief seems routinely to turn into rage. Almost every week now, in America, someone responds to his inchoate dissatisfaction with his life (it is almost always a "he") by killing strangers, sometimes by the dozen. One of them existed so completely at absolute zero that he could sit through a Bible study class with his victims, then go ahead and kill them. And I suspect many of us, myself included, can remember times when, on a smaller but still almost unbearable scale, whatever was gnawing at us from within made us cruel to those we loved best.

I once heard the great Zen teacher Thich Nat Hanh take issue with the recommendation, in some American self-help books, that it is always better to express anger. That, he said, only produces further anger, as each side more and more distorts their version of the story. Instead, he recommends simply sitting with the feeling in meditation, until it gradually transforms into something else. (This of course is not the same thing as repressing the feeling of anger; rather, it is a matter of going deeper into what lies behind it.)

Rilke writes in the *Sonnets to Orpheus*: "Killing too is a form of our wandering mourning" (II, XI, my translation). We mourn the fact that we will die, as well as all the losses, the hurts, the failures to satisfy our yearnings, we have incurred from the world outside us. Our impulse then is to turn all that outward, to destroy others as we have been or will be destroyed. Perhaps this impulse has even darker, deeper roots, in some unfathomable atavism, Darwinian struggle or Freudian death-instinct. But the fact that it can be alleviated through living with it in meditation, as Thich Nat Hanh recommends, or in the work of mourning, at least suggests that it is not the deepest level of the soul. That level might even be, as Dante and the mystics believed, "the love that moves the sun and the other stars" (*Paradiso XXXIII*, l. 145).

IV

AMBITION

TO COME AT LAST TO THE THIRD BEAST: THE SHE-WOLF, "ALL THE WORLD'S CRAVINGS"—ALL OUR DESIRES FOR THINGS TO BE DIFFERENT FROM THE WAY THEY ARE. One of our cravings, surely, is ambition: the desire to accomplish something extraordinary, to become famous and be remembered after we are dead. Ambition in the arts—though not, perhaps, in politics or high finance—is generally considered one of the more benign forms of craving. But it, too, as we shall see, poses its own problems.

Night journey stories are generally told about people who will, in the end, do something remarkable, to make their stories worth recounting. But even in these cases, there will be a preliminary period of darkness. No one knows in advance that they will do something out of the ordinary. The odds are against it. And the very conception of such an undertaking must bring with it a huge doubt of one's own capacities. If one reveals the ambition to others, one will only be ridiculed for grandiosity.

But if the fear of failure and inadequacy in the face of a grand project is part of the dark period, so too is fear of success. Large undertakings—even if they do not involve journeying to the afterlife and seeing the face of God!—involve a break from, and a competition with, the revered prior makers who should not be challenged, whether they are our specific fathers or mentors, or culture and church. Who do I think I am, to undertake such a thing? Am I not putting myself on the level of the gods? If I undertake it too soon, or perhaps even at all, will not my wings be clipped?

Or melted. The classic story about overreaching ambition is the story of Dedalus and Icarus. To escape their captivity under King Minos in Crete, Dedalus fashions wings of feathers and wax for himself and his son Icarus. He warns Icarus not to fly either too high or too low: if too low, the sea vapor will dampen his wings; if too high, the sun will melt them. But

Icarus can't resist soaring skyward. His wings fall off, and he falls into the sea.

Joyce's Stephen Dedalus thinks a great deal about the connection his name (which, of course, Joyce has invented!) gives him to the "fabulous artificer." When he leaves Dublin for Paris at the end of *A Portrait of the Artist as a Young Man*, he is convinced that his namesake will "stand me now and ever in good stead." But when he must return to Dublin, having accomplished essentially nothing as a writer, he realizes Icarus is his true parallel. He must plunge deeper into his inner darkness, before he can find a real voice.

There is reason to believe Dante had long contemplated a very grand project. At the end of the Vita Nuova, he speaks of a mysterious "vision" he has been given, and says, "it is my hope that I shall yet write concerning her [Beatrice] what has not before been written of any woman." But when Virgil actually confronts Dante with the summons to his task, Dante is stricken with self-doubt. He recalls earlier literary accounts of journeys to the afterlife. But they were vouchsafed to men who already had great missions to fulfill: Aeneas, the founder of Rome; St. Paul, the "Chosen Vessel" who brought Christianity to the Gentiles.

> But I—what cause, whose favor, could send me forth
>> On such a voyage? I am no Aeneas or Paul:
>> Not I nor others think me of such worth,
>
> And therefore I have my fears of playing the fool
>> To embark on such a venture.
>
> *(Inferno* II, ll. 25–9)

Vergil's answer is twofold. First, he simply reproaches Dante with "Cowardice." But it is the second argument that truly persuades Dante: that Beatrice, aided by St. Lucy, has come to Vergil in Limbo to tell him to lead Dante through the afterlife. At this news,

> As flowers bent and shrunken by night at dawn
>> Unfold and straighten on their stems, to wake
>> Brightened by sunlight, so I grew strong again.
>
> *(Inferno* II, ll. 103–5)

I think any of us who have conceived of grand projects can identify with both sides of Virgil's reply. We feel frustration at having conceived the project but not daring to carry it through, and accuse ourselves of cowardice. But if we are lucky—and even if we are not believing Christians—we may feel that something beyond ourselves, something in the universe that loves us, is urging us forward. We may call it divine grace; we may call it the universe's drive to self-realization. But we feel an immense reassurance when it is there.

And perhaps, psychologically speaking, all these things have their roots in infancy. For the child, setting out on one's own—even taking the first few steps away from the parent—is an enormous adventure. But, in turning one's back on the parent, there is the risk of losing the parent. If the parent immediately encourages the child, and greets the effort lovingly, all is well. But if the parent withdraws, or offers anxiety or disapproval, the child will be permanently stricken with guilt and fear at any independent action.

And so in Dante we have, on the one hand, the sense of being loved and supported by Beatrice and St. Lucy, and on the other, his fear of blasphemous presumption if he a attempts too much on his own. These issues are not simply resolved in Canto II; they persist right up to Paradiso XXXIII, as we shall see.

Early on in Inferno, we encounter two famous celebrations of human powers on their own, which Dante regards with increasing ambivalence. Inferno XV, the famous Canto of Brunetto Latini, is the second instance, after Paolo and Francesca, in which Dante regrets finding a soul in Hell, and even seems to question God's justice.

The reader may be surprised that I have not addressed this canto in the chapter on love. Dante's mentor, Ser Brunetto, is in Hell for his homosexuality. With the other sodomites, he must run forever on a burning plain. As we have seen, the perpetual motion echoes the punishment of Paolo and Francesca—in both cases, an emblem of looking for the satisfaction of ultimate love where it cannot be found.

But Ser Brunetto's conversation with Dante has little to do with sexuality, much more with what makes Ser Brunetto—unbeknownst to Dante, of course—a forerunner of the Renaissance of a century later, in his belief that humanity has an innate splendor independent of the divine. Dante says to his old teacher: "You taught me, patiently, it was you who showed

/ The way man makes himself eternal" (*Inferno* XV, ll. 81–2). "Man makes himself eternal." He does it on his own; there is no need for divine grace or support. And the word "eternal," here, has nothing to do with salvation or the afterlife. Ser Brunetto's *Tesoro*, the book for which he begs Dante's remembrance and approval, makes clear that we become eternal through great accomplishments and lasting fame.

There may indeed be a connection between Ser Brunetto's deeper sin and the sin for which he is punished. The Renaissance, like the Greco-Roman period it emulated, was much more tolerant of homosexuality than other epochs have been. Perhaps the sense of an innate beauty in our humanity goes along with the sense that erotic attachment need not be limited to the purposes of procreation.

Be that as it may, Dante at this point is entirely sympathetic to, even identified with, Ser Brunetto. The concluding simile of the canto is justly famous:

> And he went off

> Seeming to me like one of those who run
> > Competing for the green cloth in the races
> > Upon Verona's field—and of them, like one

> Who gains the victory, not one who loses.

> (*Inferno* XV, ll. 118–12)

Ser Brunetto's punishment is turned into a triumph. The runners, who according to tradition ran naked, suggest both homoerotic desire and, more largely, the Greco-Roman athleticism that glorified male beauty and strength. Robert Lowell's imitation of this canto, published in *Near the Ocean,* renders the line "who run for the green cloth through the green field." The doubled "green"—which would surely be there subliminally in the reader's mind to begin with—makes the whole scene a pastoral idyll, a kind of paradise, but a paradise entirely of this world.

It has become fashionable, among professional Dante scholars, to suggest that Dante's regret is insincere, because he himself "outed" Ser Brunetto. There are no other contemporary accounts of Brunetto's homosexuality. This argument has always seemed to me shallow, in its understanding of the artistic process. Perhaps Dante knew something about his old teacher that others did not, and was using his poetry to work through his mixed feelings. But now it seems to me that Ser Brunetto *has* to be in Hell, because his kind of humanistic pride is a stage that Dante must outgrow. Dante's regret at doing so, however, is perfectly sincere.

For Dante will show much more ambivalence toward humanist affirmation when it next rears its head, in the equally famous canto of Ulysses. The hero of the Odyssey (which Dante knew of only by reputation) is a villain in Dante's scheme of things. Dante sides with the Trojans, the putative ancestors of the Romans. So Ulysses is damned as a "false counselor," for the Trojan horse and other ingenious deceptions.

But, as with Ser Brunetto, or with Ugolino, the sin for which Ulysses is condemned plays only a minor role in the episode. Instead, Dante has invented for Ulysses a final voyage into the South Atlantic, for the sheer purpose of exploration. (Tennyson took up and expanded this story in his famous "Ulysses.")

Ulysses' speech encouraging his men toward this final adventure is justly celebrated. Primo Levi recited it to a fellow prisoner on a sunny day in Auschwitz, and it restored to both of them a minimal sense of human worth.

> Consider well your seed:
> You were not born to live as a mere brute does,
>
> But for the pursuit of knowledge and the good.
>
> (*Inferno* XXVI, ll. 113–15)

But in the narrative context, this lofty humanism is another piece of Ulysses' false counseling. It leads to his own and his entire crew's deaths. For they attempt to exceed the limits of knowledge permitted to mortals. Far in the southern seas, they approach a mountain which, as we will learn later, is Purgatory itself. To prevent their arriving there, God (referred to here as "an Other") summons a storm and a whirlpool to swallow up their ship.

Does Dante feel implicated in Ulysses' fate? How, in a way, could he not, as he too undertakes an unprecedented journey, as a mortal, onto the terrain of the afterlife? He never says he is haunted by Ulysses' presumption, but certain images recur that are, at the least, suggestive. Chief among them is the image of the boat, which reappears whenever Dante embarks on a new stage of his journey.

> To course on better waters the little
> boat of my wit, that leaves behind her
> so cruel a sea, now raises her sails.
>
> (*Purgatorio* I, ll. 1–3)

Curiously, the boat image is often accompanied by references to figures from classical mythology who were punished for competing with the gods. Here it is the "miserable magpies," the daughters of the king of Macedonia, who challenged the Muses to a singing contest. They were transformed into birds after the contest was won by Calliope, the Muse of epic poetry. And it is Calliope to whom Dante appeals, to vouchsafe that his account is divinely inspired and not, like the magpies', in competition with the gods.

The boat image occurs again in Paradiso II, as Dante warns his listeners of the dangers of the journey.

> Oh you who follow in your little bark
>   Behind my craft that finds its way by singing,
>   Desirous and attentive—Oh, turn back
>
> To see your native shore, for fear that losing
>   Sight of my wake, out there on the great waters,
>   You lose yourselves, and stay forever wandering.
>
> The gulfs I sail were never sailed before;
>   Minerva breathes on me, Apollo pilots,
>   With the nine Muses pointing out the Bears.
>
> You few, however, who long since stretched out
>   Your necks for the bread of the angels, knowing well
>   It is our life yet leaves us here, insatiate,

You too to the high salt may set your sail
    With confidence, sure you hold my furrow
    Before the waters close and make all equal.

                    (*Paradiso* II, ll. 1–15)

There are surely echoes of Ulysses' voyage in this warning. The *alto sale* (high salt) bears more than an adjectival resemblance to Ulysses' *alto mare aperto* (deep open seas, in Pinsky's version). And the waters that "close and make all equal," while literally closing in in Dante's wake, suggest the water that closed over Ulysses' ship.

    True, there is no classical instance of competition with the gods here. But the most astonishing example of that in the entire Commedia comes in the preceding canto, Paradiso I. The entire opening invocation deserves to be examined at length; it is one of the most telling instances anywhere of Dante's vacillation between human self-confidence and submission to the divine.

The glory of the one who moves all things
    Penetrates the universe, and shines out
    In one part less, another more. That ring

Of heaven that most receives His light
    I entered, and saw things that, descending here,
    I lost the knowledge or power to repeat,

Because, approaching near to its desire,
    Our intellect sinks so deep within itself
    That memory has no way to follow there.

But what of the holy realm I could carry off
    As the treasure of my inmost mind, is matter
    For this last canticle. And if,

O good Apollo, for this final labor,
    You make me such a vessel of your worth
    As only you can shape, as you require

For your beloved laurel—O on both
    Horns of Parnassus let me stand, till now
    Content with one. Apollo, come and breathe

Within my chest, even as when you drew
    Marsyas out of the scabbard of his skin.
    Lend yourself to me, O divine virtue,

Enough that the blessed kingdom's shadow-imprint
    On my brain may be manifest; and to your tree
    You will see me come, and shape myself the crown

Of which the theme, and you, shall make me worthy.
    So seldom, father, have its leaves been gathered
    For Caesar's or for poet's triumph—so faulty

And shame-abashed our human will—the venture
    Itself, the longing even, must surely make
    More joy in the joyful Delphic god. If ever,

A great flame followed from a little spark,
    Men after me may pray with truer words,
    And fail less often of the higher peak.

                               (*Paradiso* I, ll. 1–36)

After the magnificent opening, Dante seems to waver between various moods. "I'll do it myself" alternates with "But only if you'll let me," and, indeed, "only if it is really *you* who are acting through me." (The "you" here is Apollo, the patron of poetry among the Olympian gods. He is, by convention, a stand in for a more Christian conception of divine inspiration. His tree is the laurel; his sacred mountain, above his shrine at Delphi, is Parnassus, the home of the Muses.)

"I'll do it myself" is of course a basic human impulse, going back to the infant's first steps away from the mother. It is a necessary impulse for any creative endeavor, and difficult for many people. But if unchecked, it can expand into megalomaniac or even tyrannical behavior. We all need at some point the feeling that we are drawing on something beyond ourselves, whether it is (for writers) the community of literary ancestors, the Muse, the audience or some form of divine inspiration, divine grace.

So let us look at two particular instances of Dante's internal conflict, in Paradiso I. Lines 23–25, taken in isolation, might seem hubris and near-blasphemy. Crowning oneself, rather than being crowned by someone else, would have been (at least before Napoleon) the worst of bad form. Though the "tree" here is Apollo's laurel, theft from a tree cannot help but recall the original crime in Eden, the desire to be as gods.

But in context, this self-assertion is framed by appeals for the god's approval. Not only is the god called to witness this ("You will see me"), but the sentence begins and ends with declarations of complete dependence: "Lend yourself to me, o divine virtue" (literally, "O power divine, if thou grant me so much of thyself"); "Of which the theme, and you, shall make me worthy."

To make things even more complicated, the god seems also, like an ambivalent father, to *require* individual achievement, and to set the standards for it:

And if,

O good Apollo, for this final labor,
   You make me such a vessel of your worth,
   As only you can shape, as you require

For your beloved laurel

Of course, Dante concedes, again the ultimate impetus, as well as the permission, comes from the god: "As only you can shape."

Now consider the extraordinary simile of Marsyas. Like the magpies in Purgatorio I, Marsyas is a warning example of mortal artists who dared in compete with the divine. Marsyas challenged Apollo himself to a singing contest; when he lost, he was flayed alive. But now, in an astonishing condensation of contradictory themes, the horrible punishment becomes the submission that will bring inspiration:

Apollo, come and breathe

Within my chest, even as when you drew
  Marsyas out of the scabbard of his skin.

(Paradiso I, ll. 18–20)

The flaying, indeed, becomes the image for the out-of-body experience, the passing beyond human nature (*trasumanar*, to quote Dante's coinage later in the canto) which the Paradiso recounts. "Scabbard" in the Italian is *vagina*. Assuming it meant "vagina" in Dante's time, as well as the more decorous "sheathe" or "scabbard" most translators, including myself, have preferred, the condensation grows even more daring: the flaying is, in effect, a second birth. Both merging with the god and (in the dream logic) accepting punishment from him, Dante is free to proceed with his extraordinary journey, not as what he has willed, but as what grace has accorded him.

But Dante also faces another problem, the problem, in T. S. Eliot's phrase, of "the purification of the motive." How far has he undertaken his great work for its own sake, to "tell of the good I found there"? And how far is he seeking literary fame, "mak[ing] himself eternal" in Ser Brunetto's way? So he must endure a scathing lesson on the vanity of ambition, on the terrace of Pride in Purgatorio.

The souls on that terrace must crawl along weighed down by heavy stones, the opposite of their exalted view of themselves in life. As it happens, the soul Dante converses with there is a fellow artist, a decorator of illuminated manuscripts named Oderisi. Immediately, Oderisi displays a humility which, as he admits, he would not have displayed while alive:

"Brother," he said, "the pages smile more
from the brushstrokes of Franco of Bologna.
The honor is all his, apart from my share.

I would not, indeed, have been so courteous
while I was living, because of the great
desire to excel, on which my heart was set."

(*Purgatorio* XI, ll. 82–7)

The "desire to excel," in the sense of "to be excellent," should differ from the desire to be better than everyone else, but in our earthly experience, the two are hard to separate. Oderisi goes on to give a sweeping and chilling peroration on "the vain glory in human powers," as seen from the perspective of eternity:

> Do you think you will have more fame if you strip away
> the flesh in age than if you die as a baby
> still babbling baby words for bread and money,
>
> after a thousand years have passed, which is shorter
> compared to eternity than the blink of an eye
> is to that circle of Heaven that turns most slowly?
>
> (*Purgatorio* XI, ll. 103–8)

So much for man making himself eternal. Of course, Dante himself has escaped, at least for seven hundred years, the implications of his prophecy. But he could not know that; in Purgatory he says, "The truth you say humbles / my heart as it should, and shrinks a great swelling in me." And later on, in the canto of Envy, he finds himself free of that sin, but deeply fearful of having to return to the terrace of Pride after his death. But in the design of the Commedia as a whole, he has passed a test that will allow him to record his progress through paradise for its own sake.

If the reunion with Beatrice falls under Joseph Cambell's rubric of the "sacred marriage," the ambition theme falls under that of "atonement with the father." Twice in Paradiso, we are reminded of stories of sons who disobeyed their fathers, or ignored their fathers' warnings. In Canto XVII, as he is about to ask his ancestor Cacciaguida about the dark prophecies concerning his future, Dante writes:

> Then I turned to him, as Phaeton to his mother—
>   That one who makes fathers wary with their sons
>   To this very day—having heard others
> Say much against him, and needing reassurance.
>
> (*Paradiso* XVII, ll. 1–3)

Phaeton asked Apollo to confirm his paternity by allowing Phaeton to drive the chariot of the sun. Unable to control the horses, Phaeton scorched the earth and set the sky on fire, until Zeus had to kill him with his thunderbolt. And Canto VIII alludes, as we have earlier, to Dedalus and Icarus: "he that flew through the air and lost his son."

So it is probably no accident that when Dante's ambitions are compared to the power to fly, the emphasis is always on its failure. Canto XXXII warns Dante against "fall[ing] back" by "beating thy wings and thinking to advance," and cautions him to rely on divine grace. And Canto XXXIII says that if he does not appeal to the Virgin Mary for grace, he is "like one / Who would fly without wings"; at the very moment of the Beatific Vision, he says "my own wings were not sufficient."

In fact, we have had many indications, throughout the poem, that the heavenly Father does indeed approve of, and underwrite, Dante's undertaking. Perhaps the most conspicuous comes as far back as Purgatorio I. When Virgil prepares Dante for his ascent, the poem says, "As pleased another." It is, of course, the phrase that marked the terrible end of Ulysses's voyage. It pleases God that Dante should arrive, as it did not please him that Ulysses should. Dante has gotten there in the right way, by the night journey, by despair and a look into the darkest sides of his own nature, not by an overweening confidence in human splendor or the human will.

And yet, and yet. The attentive reader will notice that the image of the boat comes back one more time, at the very end, in Paradiso XXXIII. Dante has just had his vision of "the universal form of this complex," the design of the world. He cannot remember the insight itself, but believes he had it "because I can feel / My joy expanding as I tell of it."

> One moment brings me more oblivion
> That five and twenty centuries brought upon
> Neptune's wonder at the Argo's shadow.

(Paradiso XXXIII, ll. 93–6)

The voyage of Jason and the Argonauts was traditionally thought to be the first time human beings ventured out on the sea. Literally, the comparison here is between Dante's forgetting his vision—his "oblivion"—and the centuries that have passed since Jason's voyage. But we can't help feeling the true parallel is between that unprecedented voyage and Dante's extraordinary journey into the presence of God. And surely the boat carries with it all its accumulated appearances, from Ulysses's blasphemous voyage through Purgatorio I and Paradiso II. And there is even a god, once again, to witness (Neptune, the classical sea god), and to be "astonished" if not affronted. It is indeed a marvelous reprise. Human ambition, though the purified ambition of those who "long since stretched out / Your necks for the bread of the angels," is not lost. It carries us on with it into the very heart of our merging with the divine.

A postscript: one of the anxieties about ambition, especially literary ambition, is how it will affect our personal lives. There is a saying, attributed to Joan Didion, "Whenever you write, somebody's ox gets gored." If we write unfavorably about living people, however disguised, or reveal secrets they would rather keep hidden, what retaliation or shaming or ostracism might await us? Dante has certainly done his share of such things in Hell and Purgatory, and in Paradiso XVII, addressing his ancestor Cacciaguida, he worries "Lest, having lost the place that I hold dearest, / I may not lose the others by my songs."

On his journey, he has "learned things which, to many, will taste so bitter / If I were to retell them, I might regret it." But he knows he is in a double-bind:

> But if I do not, I fear to lose the future;
>> When the time comes that will call these times ancient,
>> A timid friend to truth will have few hearers.
>
> (*Paradiso* XVII, ll. 118–20)

Cacciaguida's response is what all writers would like to hear:

> Put aside all falsehood, and make plain your vision.

> And let them scratch, wherever they find an itch.
>> The food that tastes most bitter is often found
>> Once digested, the most fit to nourish.

> This cry of yours shall go as goes the wind,
>> That strikes the hardest on the highest places,
>> And this does no small honor to your mind.
>
> (*Paradiso* XVII, ll. 127–36)

In our own time, for good or bad—unless we live in dictatorships!—the danger is not so much of incurring the enmity of the powerful. It is the much more painful possibility of hurting those we love, or violating their sense of boundaries, as our writings have become increasingly personal. So we have to walk a much finer tightrope. But Dante's injunction continues to apply to us. If we do not tell essential—as opposed to merely circumstantial—truths, when delving more deeply into psychological or relational subjects than our predecessors have done, we too must fear that the times that "will call these times ancient" will have little interest in what we had to say.

V

THE TREMULOUSNESS OF RECOVERY

EVEN WITH A WORK AS FAMILIAR AND CANONICAL AS THE *DIVINE COMEDY*, INDIVIDUAL READERS MAY HAVE THEIR OWN IDIOSYNCRATIC FAVORITE SECTIONS. One of mine is the opening section of *Purgatorio*, the "Antepurgatory," where those who have not repented soon enough on earth must wait, for as long as they have lived unrepentant, to be allowed to enter the terraces of Purgatory proper, where the true process of redemptive suffering takes place. I'm partial to these cantos partly, I think, because, as W. S. Merwin has noted, Purgatory is the only section of the Commedia that takes place on the surface of this earth. We feel the softness of the air, follow the changing qualities of the sunlight as the day passes, see the shadow which Dante, as a living man, casts, and the bodiless spirits do not. And this, of course, is in enormous contrast to the darkness or monochromatic half-light, the unchangingly stale, fetid air we have just left behind in Hell. The souls' pleasure in the new sensations becomes, in Eliot's phrase, an "objective correlative" for the souls' wonder and delight in realizing that they are not, after all, damned—that their sufferings, however painful, will lead them toward salvation. We feel the enormous relief anyone feels who has emerged from a period of darkness in their lives—whether illness, external misfortune or melancholia—and, after what seems an eternity, can enjoy the simple sensations of being alive.

But with the relief comes a certain tremulousness. What if it were all to vanish, as abruptly as it came? What if the dark perspective we have endured for so long were our deepest, truest reality?

Of course, this cannot literally apply to the souls in Dante. Once they have arrived in Purgatory, they know they are saved, once and for all, however many centuries they must stay there. That is settled fact. Yet there's a timorous quality to these souls, uncertain of the terms of their new realm that for me resonates deeply with the uncertainties and fears many of us have experienced during our less firmly grounded returns to health, of whatever kind. And this contributes to the poignancy which is a ground-note of the Antepurgatory cantos, alongside the joy of the sunlight, which mirrors, perhaps, the hope of finding a fundamental goodness within the self.

The difference between Hell and Purgatory shows itself immediately as a matter of poetic making. Toward the bottom of Inferno, Dante writes:

> *S'io avesse le rime aspre e chiocce*
> *Come si converebbe al tristo buio*
> *Sovra'l qual pontan tutte l'altre rocce*

This reads, in Robert Pinsky's translation,

> If I had harsh and grating rhymes, to befit
> That melancholy hole which is the place
> All the other rocks converge and thrust their weight.
>
> (*Inferno* XXXII, ll. 1–3)

In the Italian, *aspre* (harsh) has a triple consonant, *chiocce* (grating) two double ones. Dante is piling on the least musical possibilities of the Italian language. In the third line above, only two syllable breaks lack the abrasive double consonants.

Consider, by contrast, a line describing the early morning sky, in the first canto of Purgatorio:

> **Dol**ce **c**olor d'**or**iental zaffi**ro**
>
> (*Purgatorio* I, l. 13)

("the tender color of oriental sapphire"). Almost all the vowels here are long. In the syllables I've bold, two long "ol"s, in a row, are transformed into two long "or"s, which change at the end of the line into "ro." There are only four double consonants, or five counting "ff," and all fall across natural syllabic breaks. Nothing *aspre e chiocce* here. The line is a musical equivalent of the undisturbed clarity of the jewel, or of the early morning sky.

Dante has placed Purgatory, we remember, on a mountain in the South Pacific. Dante and Virgil arrive there, through a cleft leading all the way up from Hell, at dawn on Easter Sunday—the hour of Christ's resurrection. Among the celestial beauties of the sky "the color of oriental sapphire," they see four brilliant stars invisible from the northern hemisphere:

> The sky seemed to rejoice in their points of fire—
> oh widowed northern country, you that are
> deprived of having any sight of them!
>
> (Purgatorio I, ll. 25–7)

Oh settentrional vedovo sito, the Italian reads. Fine as it is, Merwin's translation doesn't quite capture the magic of the grand, sonorous old word for north, *settentrional*, in its sound-play with *sito* (place, site). The allegorical commentators will tell us that these stars stand for the four cardinal virtues. But some have suggested that Dante had heard of the Southern Cross, from Marco Polo's voyages—an explanation I find much more charming.

The poem continues to chart the gradations of the dawn, with an attentiveness that bespeaks the delight of being once again on the surface of the earth. With the "dawn […] overcoming the pallor of daybreak," Dante can see something he could not see before, the slight motion, the "trembling of the sea" (*il tremolar de la marina*). (*Purgatorio* I, ll. 115–17; it is from the last line that I take my chapter title, though I have bent it to a psychological meaning.) Then, just before sunrise, there is a change in the colors in the sky, for which Dante finds a wonderful metaphor of aging:

> The white and vermilion cheeks
> Of lovely dawn, in the place where I was,
> Were growing old and turning orange

Finally, just rising, "On all sides the sun was firing arrows / of day" (*Purgatorio* II, ll. 7–9, 55–6).

But beyond weather and its equivalent, psychic weather, Canto I gives Dante his first assurance of redemption, and his first lesson in the dynamic process of recovery. Dante and Virgil have just encountered the first guard of Purgatory, Cato, taken from ancient Roman history to embody the stern moral code that will determine Dante and Virgil's worthiness. When

Virgil has satisfied Cato's demands, Cato assigns him two tasks, which will be the beginning of Dante's regeneration. The first is to wash Dante's face with the morning dew. When he does so, the "color" of Dante's face is "made visible once again"; thanks to "tears" as well as "dirt," he himself has been absorbed into the monochrome of Hell (*Purgatorio* I, ll. 96, 127–9).

The second task is to bind Dante's waist with a particular reed. And here, I think, we find a metaphor that resonates with all experiences of recovery:

> This little island, in the lowest places
> around it, down there where the wave beats
> upon it, bears on the soft mud rushes.

> No other plant that might make leaves or stiffen
> would be able to stay alive there
> because it would not bend under the pounding.

(Purgatorio I, ll. 100–5)

The positive counterpart to "tremulousness" is flexibility. It is perhaps the most important quality for the recovering spirit to acquire. For if the plant "stiffened"—if it tensed up, or offered the least resistance—it would immediately be broken by the vicissitudes of life that confront it. We might carry the metaphor one step further and take "stiffen[ing]" to imply any clinging to a fixed sense of self, or a fixed determination of the will. Even to think of "mak[ing] leaves," of any active resolution or new project, would be premature. It is only by complete acceptance that the rush survives in territory (implicitly, psychic territory) where nothing else could. It also has remarkable powers of self-healing. When Virgil breaks off one to bind Dante's waist, "Oh wonder!" another immediately is "reborn" in its place.

For the reader familiar with Inferno, this last section of Canto I is full of echoes and corrections. At the very beginning of his journey Dante had experienced—passively, as if it had nothing to do with his own agency—that "the true path was lost." Now Dante and Virgil seem "like someone who has found the lost road again, / who until then seems to have traveled in vain" (*Purgatorio* I, ll. 119–20).

Similarly, in Inferno XXVI, Ulysses, attempting to reach the island of Purgatory by his own will, is shipwrecked "as pleased another." The reference is to God, who is never spoken of by name in Hell. But here, when Virgil binds Dante with the reed it is "as pleased another" (*Purgatorio* I, l. 133). It pleases God that Dante, taking on the humility symbolized by the reed, should see Purgatory as part of his redemptive journey; it did not please Him that Ulysses should get there by the force of his own will.

With the second canto comes the arrival of the new souls, and Dante's reunion with his old friend the musician Casella. Dante asks Casella to sing his setting of one of Dante's own love poems, and all the shades are spellbound with delight until Cato bursts in, furious and scolding. We've already looked at this passage in Chapter II, for the light it sheds on romantic love and its relation to art. Here we might look at it in a different way, also dialectical. In recovery we all sometimes need a stern taskmaster like Cato, one who looks, as Kierkegaard put it, with "a skeptical and imploring look" at our protestations that we are doing our best, that "One does what one can" (Kierkegaard, p. 345). But such injunctions alone cannot give us the feeling of joy we need to bear up under the ordeal. For that we, like the souls, need the rare moments when we can feel "as content as though / there was nothing else touching [our] minds" (*Purgatorio* II, ll. 116–17).

For the task can seem almost impossible at first. When Dante and Virgil reach the first set of cliffs surrounding the mountain,

> we found the rock face was so steep
> that nimbleness of legs would have been in vain.

> Between Lerici and Turbia, the most naked place,
> where the scree is broken smallest, is a spacious
> and gradual staircase compared to this.
>
> (*Purgatorio* III, ll. 46–51)

It almost seems that "here one has to fly" (*Purgatorio* IV, l. 27).

And when they reach a cleft where they can climb, its opening seems so narrow that

> Often the peasant closes a wider breach
> in the hedge with a forkful of his sloe-thorns
> at the season where the grapes begin to darken.
>
> (*Purgatorio* IV, ll. 19–21)

But when Dante emerges at the top, exhausted, Virgil reassures him:

> It is the way of this mountain
> always to seem hard at the beginning
> and become easier as one goes on climbing.
>
> (*Purgatorio* IV, ll. 88–90)

It is a familiar truth, almost a truism, about the process of recovery.

The Casella passage also introduces an important and poignant repeated metaphor: the comparison of the souls in Antepurgatory, in their tremulous uncertainty, to docile, even simple-minded animals. Just after Cato's scolding, the souls running away toward the mountain are compared to doves. We've already seen how this echoes and, in a way, redeems, the dove metaphor applied to Paolo and Francesca in *Inferno* V. But we might also notice the homely, almost comical, aspect of the passage:

> As doves when they are picking up wheat or weed seeds
> all together, quietly feeding
> without their usual puffed-up displaying,
>
> if something should appear that frightens them
> suddenly abandon what had tempted them,
> seized as they are by what matters more to them,
>
> so I saw that fresh troop abandon
> the singing and wheel away toward the slope
> like one who goes without knowing the direction.
>
> (*Purgatorio* II, ll. 124–32)

The doves, here, freed of their egos, "their usual puffed-up displaying," are so timorous that they fly away "without knowing the direction," or knowing what it is that has frightened them. And they act as a group; there is no individual initiative.

Both the timidity, and the uniform group behavior, recur in Canto III, when Dante and Virgil encounter a group of souls, who draw back frightened when they catch sight of them. Again, there's a wonderful animal simile:

60

As the sheep make their way out of the fold
one, then two, then three, and the rest stay behind
timid, with eyes and noses to the ground,

and whatever the first one does the others do,
piling on top of it if it stops,
simple and quiet and without knowing why,

so I saw the van of that fortunate flock
make a movement toward us, modesty
in their features, and stepping with dignity.

(Purgatorio III, ll. 79–87)

Certainly, there's more comedy here: the sheep that follow piling on the top of the first one when it stops. Nevertheless, there is "modesty" and "dignity" in the souls' surrender of their individual wills, as they proceed, "simple and quiet and without knowing why." Perhaps, to draw the analogy with our own experiences of recovery, in our earlier lives we may have told ourselves too many half-true stories about "why" we are doing the things we are doing. Letting go of our certainties regarding the future forces us to react only to the moment immediately facing us, even if those reactions seem foolish to an ignorant observer.

Nor is the submergence of individual in group identity necessarily a bad thing. One might think of the premises of AA meetings and their essential humility: "I'm Joe, I'm an alcoholic." Acknowledging that one's experience belongs to a general human category frees one from attaching too much importance to our idiosyncratic personal histories in trying to explain our predicament. Beyond that, all of this might fall under the rubric of what some psychoanalysts have called "regression in the service of ego-integration." Our sheep-like, passive acceptance may be the cocoon from which the active individual will may reemerge, founded on firmer ground.

(This may be the place to note that, though there will be some reference to twelve-step programs, my sense of "recovery" does not refer primarily to them. It refers to all experiences of emergence from the dark night, whether though psychotherapy or simply one's own resources.)

For us, the timidity the souls experience might be occasioned in part by our fear of falling back into our earlier hell-like state. For the souls in Purgatory, as we've seen, there is no such danger (though there might be for Dante himself). But there are a couple of curious facts about Purgatory that do seem to adumbrate such a fear, on the subliminal level. The first is the strange rule, revealed in Canto IX, according to which it is impossible to move upward on the mountain, by so much as an inch, after nightfall. But it is easy to stray back downward. So Dante and Virgil are told to find a peaceful place to rest, and stay there. Night is, of course, the domain of the unconscious, of dreams. So the rule suggests that in that realm we are still prey to all the old demons and temptations. We need the rational clarity of daylight to continue to make progress.

Stranger still is the episode that follows this injunction. Toward the twilight of their first day in Purgatory, Dante and Virgil, temporarily accompanied by the soul of the poet Sordello, reach a place called the Valley of the Kings. It is the most beautiful place we have yet seen in the Commedia, or will see until we reach the Earthly Paradise. A hollow in the upward sweep of the mountain, it is covered with grass and spring flowers, which Dante compares to a jeweled inlay. On my visits to Tuscany, in spring and even into late summer, there are hundreds of beautiful small flowers scarcely higher than the grass; I have seen nothing like it anywhere else in the world. So the inlay image is, once again, exact.

In their beautiful valley, waiting to enter Purgatory proper, we find the well-intentioned kings and princes who have allowed evil to persist by neglecting some aspect of their duties. As twilight comes on in their beautiful valley, they all begin to sing the hymn *Te lucis ante* (Before the ending of the day). But now comes the very strange episode. Two angels appear, dressed completely in green and armed with flaming swords, at the heights of either side of the valley, protectively "containing" its inhabitants. Sordello explains that they have come "to protect the valley / because of the serpent that before long you will see" (*Purgatorio* VIII, ll. 38–9). And soon enough "the adversary," as Sordello calls him, appears:

> On that side where the small valley has
> no ramparts was a snake. Maybe it was

that kind that gave the bitter food to Eve.
   Through the grass and flowers came the streak of evil,
turning its head to the side, and again, and again,
licking its back like a preening animal.

   I did not see and so I cannot tell
of the motion of the celestial
falcons, though I saw them both plainly in motion.

   Hearing the green wings split the air, the serpent
fled.

(Purgatorio VIII, ll. 97–107)

Much thought has been lavished on the allegory here, especially since
Dante tells us it ought to be easy to understand:

   Reader, sharpen your eyes here to see
the truth, for now the veil is certainly
so fine that passing through it will be easy.

(Purgatorio VIII, ll. 19–21)

Readers, in general, have not found it so. But in psychological terms, the
matter seems both simpler and sadder. There is always a side of our mind
that "has / no ramparts." As Freud says, once the track of a symptom or
obsessive idea has been laid down in the brain, it is there forever. Sadly, it
is often at the moments when we are happy enough that our guard is down
that we sense and fear it again—fear that it is our deepest reality. The old
serpent always comes back again. But in recovery we have "angels" to drive
it away, though we do not know by what "motion" they do so. It is not a
matter of our conscious insight, our conscious will. And it is important
that the angels' robes and wings are green. Green is, iconographically, the
color of hope. Perhaps Dante is suggesting that we are proof against the
power of the serpent because we have learned to hope, not because of anything we know or believe.

   With the Valley of the Kings we leave behind Antepurgatory, and the
note of poignancy that pervades it. Nowhere is that note so beautifully
expressed as in the opening lines of Canto VIII:

63

Then it was the hour that brings longing again
to melt the hearts of those out on the sea
the day they have said goodbye to their dear friends,

and when love stabs the new pilgrim who hears
far off in the distance a bell ringing
as though mourning the day that is dying.

(Purgatorio VIII, ll. 1–6)

The passage conveys, for the first and last time in the Commedia, the sadness we must feel at leaving the familiar past behind, with its beloved inhabitants—whether we are seafarers facing new dangers, or, like Dante, "pilgrims" who know that the ultimate goal is to be preferred. It is our last experience of the poignancy of purely human time. In Purgatory proper, there will be no more nostalgia. When the gate of Purgatory clangs shut behind him, Dante is told, if he looks back for so much as an instant, he will find himself outside again.

Here we might leave Dante, except that the structure of Purgatory, as opposed to that of Hell, has something more to teach us about psychological and spiritual progress. Hell is classified according to *acts*, and sets out to demonstrate which acts are worse than others, according to an Aristotelian-Thomistic schema. Purgatory, however, is organized by the medieval categories of the seven deadly sins. And these sins are essentially *motives*: pride, envy, anger, sloth, avarice, gluttony, lust.

The difference bears an analogy, I think, to the therapeutic process. At the beginning a patient—some patients, anyway—may repeat over and over, "I did this and that terrible thing." S/he is totally in the grip of the accusatory superego, and in that grip feels hopeless, damned. But at a certain point the therapist may say, "But *why* did you do it?" And here, as in Purgatory, the focus changes. There is the possibility of growth, for if the motive is deeply understood, the patient is less likely to commit similar acts again. Indeed, in the very moment of pondering the question, the patient is able to view the act with a certain mental detachment—to be curious what the act means, as a human manifestation, rather than what it says about his own essential nature. The patient doesn't stop feeling guilty, but the increase in self-understanding brings with it a bit of self-compassion. And there is also a sense of commonality with the rest of humanity, since motives, unlike deeds or symptoms, are universal.

The journey through Purgatory seems all the more therapeutic because Dante must, to some degree, undergo the punishment for the sins of which he finds himself particularly guilty. Purgatory is so organized that he can pass through the terraces of envy, sloth, avarice and gluttony as a disinterested spectator. But in the canto of anger, as we have already seen, Dante must suffer the suffocating smoke along with all the souls there, and it seems almost worse to him than Hell. In the circle of lust, Dante must pass through the wall of fire where the souls are imprisoned, so hot that "I would have thrown / myself into boiling glass to be cooler" (*Purgatorio* XXVII, ll. 49–50).

The same thing happens in the cantos of pride, though in a subtler way. The souls of the arrogant, as we have seen, must walk bent double, almost to the ground, to carry the heavy stones on their backs. When Dante first glimpses them, they seem to him scarcely human. But he himself must bend down to their level to talk to them, sharing that sub-humanity, so that he and the afflicted spirit seem like "oxen yoked together" (*Purgatorio* XII, l. 1). It happens that the spirit Dante is so "yoked" with is the illuminator Oderisi. And so he receives the lecture, so germane to his own occasions for pride, on the vanity of the yearning for fame, which we have examined in Chapter IV. And he must absorb that lesson, before he can stand up again to his full height.

Dante, as a medieval Christian, believes that he will have to pass through Purgatory again after his death. But we as readers experience his journey as a true and valid purgation. And indeed, this inference is built into the text itself. Extraordinarily, the angel at the gateway marks Dante's brow with seven P's, just as he does with the souls who have come there after death. And when Dante rises from his crouched position in the circle of pride, an angel appears and touches Dante's forehead with his wings. Immediately one of the P's disappears, and Dante feels that "a heavy / thing has been lifted from [him]." Perhaps it is the stone of pride. He walks on, as Virgil had predicted earlier, "feel[ing] almost no effort in it" (*Purgatorio* XII, ll. 118–20). And the ascent itself has become easier; no longer a cleft in the rock, it is a "sacred stair" (*Purgatorio* XXII, l. 115).

Whatever Dante's theological beliefs, in the archetypal terms of the night journey, Purgatory completes his journey of self-discovery. Hell has shown him the worst possibilities of human nature, and the potential for them within himself. Purgatory has given him the understanding of his own motives, and with it the possibility of self-compassion. He is now ready for the sacred marriage, the reunion with Beatrice. But before that happens, Virgil says to him, in the words we have already considered in Chapter II,

> Expect no further word or sign from me.
> Your own will is whole, upright, and free,
> and it would be wrong not to do as it bids you,
>
> therefore I crown and miter you over yourself.
>
> (Purgatorio XXVII, ll. 139–42)

It is what a good psychoanalyst might say at the end of a long analysis. The patient is not promised a life free of misfortunes or mental vicissitudes. But there is the assurance that the patient can face them confidently, not subject to his or her own moods or impulses, but able to rule over them, to make decisions freely and with a certain inner detachment. And it is in that state that we leave Dante, "pure and ready to ascend to the stars" (*Purgatorio* XXXIII, l. 145).

VI

IDENTITY IN PARADISE

IN EUGENIO MONTALE'S "XENIA," THE POET'S COMPANION, HAVING JUST TASTED A WINE CALLED "INFERNO," ASKS, "IS THERE A PARADISO TOO"? The waiter replies:

> "I think so, Signora, but nobody likes
> those sweet dessert wines anymore."

(Montale, p. 303)

Most readers of Dante, it is undeniable, stop with Inferno. A substantial minority will go on to Purgatorio, especially now that we have Merwin's translation to carry over its lyrical magic into English. But few indeed take on Paradiso.

There are clear reasons for this. Wallace Stevens's typical view of the conventional Christian heaven as a place where we "pick the strings of our insipid lutes" infects our expectations of any depiction of it, even from a poet as great as Dante. And it is notoriously hard for art to portray goodness and happiness, without the contrasts, the pungency, of more mixed experience.

Moreover, one might say, the other cantiche have fairly constant analogues in our lives. Purgatory is our daily experience; we can visit Hell by opening any newspaper. Paradise we experience briefly if at all: a walk in early spring; an intense conversation with someone we are falling in love with; a few serene hours during a long meditation retreat. Perhaps we receive an extraordinary kindness from someone we come to regard as a saint. And it may be that, as Wordsworth says, "Heaven lies about us in our infancy," but so do darker experiences, and our memory of both is fragmentary.

Still, there is some dissent. James Merrill, in his *Book of Ephraim*, contends that the visionary visit to Heaven is the only part of the Commedia that Dante authentically experienced:

> The resulting masterpiece takes years to write;
> More, since the dogma of its day
> Calls for a Purgatory, for a Hell,
> Both of which Dante thereupon, from footage
> Too dim or private to expose, invents.
> His Heaven, though, as one cannot but sense,
> Tercet by tercet, is pure Show and Tell.

(Merrill, p. 45)

Merrill's claim rests on the exceedingly peculiar "dogma" of his own Ouija-board afterlife. Nevertheless, the argument could be supported on more conventional grounds. The premonitory dream, in the *Vita Nuova*, that leads Dante to say he will write of Beatrice "what has never been written of any woman" is of a visit to Heaven. Hell and Purgatory are not mentioned in it.

Without going as far as Merrill, I would like to speak up for the some of the splendors of the *Paradiso*. Aside from some long-winded stretches of history and medieval philosophy, it is beautifully written, especially in the imagery of light. And it provides as vivid an account as I know of experiences that seem to stretch the boundaries of our consciousness—the *trasumanar* (going beyond the human) which, Dante says, language can barely approach.

Of all these experiences, I'm going to focus on those that involve our sense of self in relation to other selves, what philosophers call the problem of "other minds." Can we acknowledge the reality of others without losing our precious sense of our own uniqueness? Can I fully exist, if others do equally? I suspect we go through much of our lives with only a rote acknowledgment of the full reality of other selves, until a moment of extraordinary intimacy occurs. And even then, we may fear losing our selves in giving the other so much power over, and insight into, our inner being. And all this is in addition to the inevitable factors of competition and envy in the Darwinian struggle over the goods of this world.

Dante, however, proposes a different economy, in which the more one feels in contact with, and understood by, others, the larger grows one's sense of one's own identity. Let me begin by offering a very small example. At the beginning of Canto III, Beatrice has just given Dante a rather severe intellectual drubbing, for his theories about the spots on the moon: "Your belief is sunk in error." But now he says, "I drew myself to my full height / To confess myself corrected" (*Paradiso* III, ll. 3–6). Such treatment, in ordinary life, often makes us feel smaller, and often makes us look for some plausible defense, rather than "confess [ourselves] corrected." But on rare occasions—most of us will remember one or two—we do accept the other person's interpretation, simply because it rings true for us inside. And then we may feel *piu erto*—both "taller" and "more straight"—because our ego has proved weaker than our larger self, which wants to be truthful. (The idiom "I stand corrected," more common in our parents' time than now, conveys the same idea.)

Such outcomes, the exception on earth, are the norm in Paradise. In Canto III, Dante will ask the spirits in the sphere of the moon, who appear to have been assigned the lowest place in heaven, somewhat naively:

> But tell me truly: do you not desire,
>> For all your happiness, a higher place
>> Where you could see more, and be held more dear?
>>>> (*Paradiso* III, ll. 64–6)

Beatrice will explain to Dante, later, that all the spirits are equally in the presence of God, and that their division is partly illusory, for his education. But, for the moment, the spirit replies:

> "Brother, not a trace
> Of will in us is not quieted, here above,
>> By charity's superabundant power;
>> We thirst for nothing more than what we have."
>>>> (*Paradiso* III, ll. 70–2)

A few lines later comes the line made famous by Matthew Arnold and T. S. Eliot: "Our peace is in His will" (*Paradiso* III, l. 85).

Dante has posed a similar question here earlier, in Purgatorio XV. It goes to the core of the issue of whether competitiveness, based on scarcity, can be overcome:

How can a good be shared out among many
so that each of them becomes richer in it
than if only a few divided it?

(Purgatorio XV, ll. 61–3)

Virgil's reply makes clear how the celestial economy differs from the earthly one. Dante goes wrong, Virgil says, because his "desires are fastened where / if there is company each part is smaller" (*Purgatorio* XV, ll. 49–50). But the "infinite and indescribable good," by contrast,

gives of itself according to the ardor
it finds, so that as charity spreads farther
the eternal good increases upon it,

and the more souls there are who love, up there,
the more there are to love well, and the more love
they reflect to each other, as in a mirror.

(Purgatorio XV, ll. 67, 70–5)

Putting it psychologically, one might say that if the experience of love or compassion, "charity," enlarges the self rather than making it feel vulnerable, as competition and envy do, then the self has more love to hand on, so there is more love in the universe. And so the spirits in the second celestial planet will say, as they approach Dante in *Paradiso* V: "Lo here comes one who will increase our loves" (*Paradiso* V, l. 105).

The English poet Shelley, himself an accomplished *dantista*, sums it up in these lines from "Epipsychidion":

True love in this differs from gold or clay,
That to divide is not to take away.

(Shelley, ed. Baker, p. 278)

We've already noticed the generosity of the spirits in the Heaven of Venus, Cunizza in particular. But this eagerness to extend welcome in fact extends to all the souls in Paradise. The same spirit in Canto V who has said "here comes one who will increase our loves," when Dante actually questions him, becomes so radiant with "happiness" that his entire visible form is swallowed up in light.

70

But there is another, stranger dimension to this whole nexus of themes. As he moves farther into Paradise, Dante becomes increasingly aware that the spirits not only welcome him eagerly; they have a kind of telepathic access to his thoughts. He refers to Beatrice as "she from whom my thoughts could not be hid." But the great efflorescence of this theme comes in Canto IX, the Heaven of Venus, which we have already examined in the chapter on love. "Give me proof," he says to Cunizza, "that what I think I can reflect on thee," and then, more astonishingly, to Folco:

> I should not wait for you to ask the question
> If I withinned-you as you within-me.
>
> (*Paradiso* IX, ll. 20–1, 80–1)

The Italian, which I have tried so awkwardly to translate here, is *s'io m'intuassi come tu t'inmii*. *M'intuassi* and *t'inmii* are neologisms, coined words that did not exist before in Italian. As Brenda Deen Schildgen points out in an excellent essay, Dante uses such coinages throughout the Paradiso to convey "the ineffable," states "for which language does not exist through concepts did." In this one, the key idea is "in." In our conventional language, where access to the consciousness of another person would imply intrusion, the person intruded on, the *tu* or *mi*, would be the object of the verb. Instead, this syllable becomes mysteriously part of the verb itself, as if being within someone else were a condition, not an action. Indeed, the direct object of the verb is the same as the subject, as if the supposed intrusion were something the actor was doing to himself: at best, "I place myself inside you."

This is what we call a reflexive construction; as Schildgen points out, such constructions are much more common in Italian than in English. In English we only use this construction where it is absolutely necessary: "I kill myself." In Italian, however, it is much more common; an Italian would say "I dress myself" where we say "I get dressed," or "I call myself" where we would say "My name is." In Dante's context, the important point is that the telepathic act is not something the spirit does to Dante, or God to the spirit, but more something the spirit does to itself. It is not "I penetrate you," which would imply aggression or domination, but at most, as we have seen, "I put myself within you," "I in-you myself." It is almost not an active verb at all, rather "I am in you." As Brenda Schildgen points out, "In many languages reflexive constructions have a passive meaning because, linguists hypothesize, in both passive and reflexive constructions, subject and object are 'non-distinct.'" She goes on to quote John Haiman as saying that "when the reflexive object is incorporated into the verb [as by the apostrophes here, *t'inmii*] this self-awareness or alienation from the self is lacking" (Schildgen, p. 113). In short, it is not only the recipient of the action, Dante, who experiences a slipping of the boundaries of self-awareness, of the ego that perceives itself as detached from everything else; simultaneously, the spirit who enters into the transaction experiences the same. As Sinclair puts it, Dante's neologisms convey "a mystery that cannot be told in common speech, no loss of personality but the fulfillment of it in an immediacy of intercourse, thought with thought, which belongs to the life of Paradise" (Sinclair, note, p. 43).

This interpenetrability of selves, in Paradise, leads us back to some of the most ancient questions. Who are we—at the innermost core? Some religions—Christianity and, to a degree, Hinduism—posit a unique, permanent soul, a "substance" in the old Aristotelian vocabulary. At the other extreme, some contemporary thinkers believe that all our images of our "self" are internalized social constructs, whirling about and banging into each other around an empty center.

The great object-relations psychoanalyst D. W. Winnicott posited a middle way. Our sense of self is real, and grounded in our ability to recognize our authentic feelings. But that ability itself originates in an interaction with an other, the mother of infancy. Winnicott's idea of maternal "mirroring" was developed in response to Jacques Lacan's thesis, the basis of the social constructionist view of selfhood, that "self-awareness," which is also "alienation from the self," begins in the encounter with literal mirrors. Winnicott claims that there is an earlier mirror, the mother's gaze, and that it can produces a sense of unity with oneself, rather than alienation:

> What does the baby see when he or she looks at the mother's face? I am suggesting that, what the baby sees is himself or herself. In other words the mother is looking at the baby and *what she looks like is related to what she sees there*. (Winnicott, p. 122)

In this reflection of the baby in what the mother "looks like," the baby's sense of having an authentic self is first validated. So Jessica Benjamin writes:

A person comes to feel that "I am the doer who does, I am the author of my acts," by being with another person who recognizes her acts, her feelings, her intentions, her existence, her independence. [...] The subject declares "I am, I do," then waits for the response, "You are, you have done." (Benjamin, p. 21)

Later theorists in the object-relations lineage, notably Benjamin herself, have developed a term for the sense of being almost inside another person's thoughts, without doing them harm or diminishing their sense of identity. These theorists call it "intersubjectivity"—a term derived from the phenomenologist Husserl, through the social theorist Habermas. This view—in contrast to a purely "intrapsychic" one, which sees the subjective world as in some sense a closed system—"maintains that the individual grows in and through the relationship with other subjects [...] . [E]ven when describing the self alone, [it] sees its aloneness as a particular point in the spectrum of relationships rather than as the original, 'natural state' of the individual" (Benjamin, p. 20). Such growth is essential, not only to our happiness in infancy, but to all our later encounters with others, including successful psychotherapy. In this, as in so much else, Dante was centuries ahead of his time.

But, of course, Dante as a medieval Christian does not question the idea of an eternal, substantial soul. But that soul, though substantial, is also contingent, on its relation with God, its creator and its omnipresent witness. This is the ultimate intersubjectivity, which makes possible all the others. In fact, the *in* neologism first appears in this context, in Paradiso III: *com'allo re ch'a suo voler ne invoglia*. This is often translated, as Sinclair does, as "the King who wills us to His will." But in fact what it says is more "the King who to his will in-wills us" (*Paradiso* III, l. 84). The implication is that God acts, or becomes present, within our wills themselves, so that we conform to his will not by an act of submission, but by transformation. We might even say it is empowering: we discover a larger will within ourselves when it is expanded by the presence of God's will. The construction recurs once more in Canto IV, this time directed from the creature to the Creator: the Seraphim who "most within-Gods himself" [*piu s'india*] (*Paradiso* IV, l. 28).

And finally it is this relation to God that makes possible intersubjectivity between people. Before the line we have already considered, "If I withinned-you as you within-me," Dante says to Folco,

Since God sees all, and your own vision so
   Withins-him […] no wish of mine
   Knows how to steal itself away from you.

(Paradiso IX, ll. 73–5)

The Italian reads: *Dio vede tutto, e tuo veder s'inluia*. It is by participating, to some degree, in the omniscience of God that the souls of the saved have inner access to other souls. And, earlier, he says to Charles Martel,

Since I believe you see, as clearly as I,
   How the words you have spoken, my dear lord,
Infuse me with the most exalted joy,
   And see it where all good things have their end
   And their beginning, I cherish that joy doubly
Because you behold it, gazing upon God.

(Paradiso VIII, ll. 85–90)

Yet it's striking how often the image of the mirror, crucial to Winnicott as to Lacan, recurs in these passages, and indeed, as we shall see, becomes central to the imagistic development of the Paradiso. In Canto IX, Cunizza justifies her harsh prophecies in these terms:

There are mirrors above us—you would call them Thrones—
   Reflecting down God in the act of judging;
   Wherefore it seems quite fitting to us to own
Such speech.

(Paradiso IX, ll. 61–3)

Soon enough, this imagery takes on its Winnicottian connection to a relation with another human being. We've seen, in Chapter II, how Beatrice's smile becomes her defining characteristic in Paradise. But as we move into the higher circles, that smile becomes more and more a look in her eyes. In Paradiso XV,

Such a smile was aglow within her eyes
   I felt my own eyes touching there
   The depth of their grace and of their paradise.

(Paradiso XV, ll. 34–6)

Mutual recognition as well as enlightenment is clearly at issue here: it is when his eyes "touch" the "depth[s]" of hers that he is in "paradise."

The poet-critic Allen Tate writes, in a remarkable essay we shall be returning to, "Beatrice's eyes [...] are the first mirror" (Tate, p. 110). He is thinking, primarily, of the passage in Purgatorio XXXI, where Dante first looks into Beatrice's eyes after their reunion:

> A thousand desires hotter than a flame
> held my eyes on those shining eyes
> that were fixed on the griffin the whole time.
>   Like the sun in a mirror, not otherwise,
> the double beast was shining in her eyes
> now with one nature, now the other.
>
> (*Purgatorio* XXXI, ll. 118–23)

The "flame" of erotic love here is transmuted into the solarity of vision. The griffin—a mythological beast, half-eagle and half-lion—represents, in Dante's allegory, the double nature of Christ. It is, therefore, by looking into Beatrice's eyes, and seeing the griffon shift back and forth between its two natures, that Dante first understands the mystery of the Incarnation. (And is Beatrice herself not an Incarnation, fleshly love on the one hand, on the other intersubjectivity not only with another human being but with Being itself?)

Psychoanalytically speaking, the experience of the mirroring look is accompanied, even preceded, by a more primordial experience of connection, that of the nursing infant. Melanie Klein writes, "[t]he relation to the gratifying breast in some measure restores, if all goes well, the lost prenatal union with the mother" (Klein, pp. 211–12). So I hope it won't seem reductive to notice how consistently Dante poses our relation to what is ultimately good—whether intellectual wisdom or mystical enlightenment—in terms of feeding. In Canto II he speaks of the "few [...] who long since stretched out / Your necks for the bread of the angels." This, of course, refers primarily to the Eucharist, but the canto goes on to speak of "That thirst, unending because created with us, / For the kingdom that shows the form of God" (*Paradiso* II, ll. 10–11, 19–20). Canto III speaks of the sweetness of "the rays of eternal life [...] [t]heir everlasting taste" (*Paradiso* III, ll. 38–9). And Beatrice herself, in Canto VII, is "my Lady who slakes my thirst with sweet drops" (*Paradiso* VII, ll. 11–12).

The act of nursing itself comes to the fore in two crucial passages near the end of Paradiso. In Canto XXX, when Dante has his first vision of the saved in the presence of God as a river lined with flowers, Beatrice tells him to drink of its waters.

> No infant, waking past its usual hour,
>   Flings its face more rapidly toward the milk
>   Than I, to make of my eyes better mirrors,
> Bent to the water.
>
> (*Paradiso* XXX, ll. 82–6)

No sooner have his eyelids touched the stream than it displays its true form, the celestial rose of the saints expanding toward the divine light.

And then in the midst of the Beatific Vision itself, Dante writes:

> From here on my tongue will fall even shorter
>   With regard to what I can remember,
>   than an infant's still bathing at the breast.
>
> (*Paradiso* XXXIII, ll. 107–9)

The surface sense is of course negative: it is the inadequacy of Dante's language that is compared to the infant, who cannot speak a single word. But the ecstasy conveyed by the word "bathing" (*bagni*) tells a different story. The first human experience of oceanic oneness becomes a subterranean metaphor for the last.

But let us return to looks and mirroring. Dante's last penetrating gaze, of course, is into the face of God himself. Beatrice has vanished unnoticed, as Virgil vanished earlier, and taken her place among the saints in the celestial rose. And so we come to Canto XXXIII, which Robert Lowell called the "most magnificent" treatment of "mystical contemplation […] in Christian literature" (Lowell, p. 218).

Instructed by St. Bernard, Dante gazes directly into the light emanating from the Godhead. The first fruit of his vision is an understanding of the order of the universe, in the terms of the philosophy of his time. I quote W. S. Merwin's translation here, and in all other citations from Paradiso XXXIII:

In its depths I saw that it contained,
   by love into a single volume bound,
   the scattered pages of the universe,

substances, accidents, and their relations
   in such a way seemed to me mingled that
   what I say is a simple glimmer of it.

He compares his journey into the light, as we have seen, to the first human voyage, the Argo's shadow that astonished the sea gods. As he sees farther in, or, as he suggests, as his power to endure what he sees increases, three circles of different colors appear. They represent, of course, the Trinity. And then, from the middle of the circle that corresponds to the Son, a human image appears. Dante struggles to understand the relation between the circle and the image, as, he says, a mathematician might struggle with the problem of squaring the circle. Then, in a "flash," he understands.

Allen Tate, in the essay I have cited, offers an extraordinary reading of this passage. Noting that the "three circles [...] *reflect*" each other (italics mine), he takes us back to an earlier image of literal mirrors. In a passage in Canto II, which is usually either overlooked on taken as an anticipation of modern science, Beatrice proposes an experiment:

Take three mirrors; have two of them set
   At an equal distance from you; in the middle
   Let the third glass be placed so as to greet
Your eye from a greater distance. Take a candle,
   And, keeping your face turned toward the three glasses,
   Have it lit behind your back to kindle
All three, so they return to you its brightness.
   You will see, though the light farthest from you shows
   Smaller, it still shines with equal brightness.

                 (*Paradiso* II, ll. 98–105)

Tate maintains that the three mirrors here prefigure the three circles of Canto XXXIII:

There are *three* mirrors reflecting the one light. In the heart of the Empyrean, as we have seen, Dante says: *In the profound and shining being of the deep light there appeared to me* three *circles of* three *colors and one magnitude* [emphasis on "three" Tate's]. In the middle is the effigy of man. The physical image of Dante had necessarily been reflected in each of the three mirrors in Canto II; but he had not then seen it. I suggest that he was not ready then to see it; his dramatic [...] development fell short of the final self-knowledge. (Tate, p. 111)

The inevitable conclusion is that the human face Dante sees at the center is not only the image of Jesus but his own reflection. This is the "final self-knowledge." But how, without blasphemy, could this be true?

C. G. Jung's writings may help us to understand. Jung uses the term "individuation" to describe a spiritual journey like Dante's, in which darker portions of our selves are recognized and assimilated into our conception of the self. But, counterintuitively, the individuated self becomes in a certain sense less individual, more universal and more like other selves, since here all the imbalances of our unique histories are corrected, all our capacities realized. Toward the end of a process of individuation, "symbols of unity and wholeness," "totality images," begin to appear in the subject's dreams or fantasies. And, Jung goes on to say, "the spontaneous symbols of the self, or of wholeness, cannot in practice be distinguished from a God-image." Ultimately,

> *Christ exemplifies the archetype of the self* [italics Jung's]. He represents a totality of a divine or heavenly kind, a glorified man. [...] As *Adam secundus* he corresponds to the first Adam before the fall, when the latter was still a pure image of God, of which Tertullian (d. 222) says, "And this therefore is to be considered as the image of God in man, that the human spirit has the same motions and senses as God has, though not in the same way as God has them." (Jung, *Aion*, p. 37)

Thus, it would seem, with Dante. In seeing Christ, he sees the end of his own journey, what Tate calls "final self-knowledge," what Jung calls the "archetype of the self." One might think, too, of Joseph Campbell's final stage of "Apotheosis," which involves a similar recognition of God in the self and the self in God.

At the end of the Commedia, Dante understands in a flash how the human face and the circle are united; that is to say, what the relation is between the "totality" of our human nature and that of the cosmos. His being in that moment of incommunicable insight is compared to "a wheel that is moved evenly"; that is to say, he is equivalent to the planetary wheels, all of them set in motion by "the Love that moves the sun and the other stars." Jung would not have been surprised by this image; the "wheel," or mandala, is another of his images for realized "totality," and in one passage he compares it to the planetary orbits. (He also adduces the squaring of the circle, mentioned in Paradiso XXXIII, l. 134, as another "totality" image.)

But enough of authorities! For we must emphasize that what Dante records is an experience, not a concept. It derives its power to convince from the *feeling* of authenticity it gives him. He says so twice, touchingly, in Canto XXXIII. First he writes,

> As one who sees when he is dreaming, and
>   after the dream the imprint of the passion
>   stays, and the rest does not come back to mind,
>
> so am I, for almost all of my
>   vision has vanished, and still the sweetness born
>   from it is distilled in my heart to me.
>
>   (*Paradiso XXXIII*, ll. 58–63)

And later, after his vision of "substances, accidents, and their relations":

> I believe I saw the universal
>   form of this knot because I can feel
>   my joy expanding as I tell of it.
>
>   (*Paradiso XXXIII*, ll. 91–3)

The *feeling*, ultimately, is what authenticates the experience. As Adrienne Rich put it, in a very different context, Dante has experienced "the wreck and not the story of the wreck."

Dante has come a long way since the dark wood. He has gone down into the "heart's lake," and into the "deep well" of Cocytus, where all evil becomes possible through the complete extinguishing of human empathy. He has survived, and purged his quest, as far as possible, from impure motives: the yearning for fame, the ego's desire to be extraordinary. He has seen his beloved, Beatrice, change from the object of romantic longing to the very manifestation of God's creative splendor. But he might not have been able to experience all this if he had not started in such a lowly place. Jung writes in *Aion*: "This increase in self-knowledge is still very rare nowadays and is usually paid for in advance with a neurosis, if not with something worse" (Jung, pp. 19–20). Perhaps it was not so rare in Dante's time, but he too, like Jung's dreamer, had to descend into the dark water before he could ascend the shining hill, could see God in himself and himself in God.

*

Sometime during the years when I was thinking about Dante, I was sitting in a doctor's waiting room and read an article in *Time* or *Newsweek* about Dr. Eben Alexander. (Dr. Alexander later wrote a book about his experience, called *Proof of Heaven*.)

Himself a highly trained and successful neurosurgeon, Dr. Alexander was in a coma for six days with an extremely rare form of bacterial meningitis. Only the most primitive parts of his brain continued to function. "The higher-level functions" in the neocortex, to which we customarily attribute consciousness, along with language, emotion, logic, were determined by neurological tests to be "entirely absent." But somewhere, Dr. Alexander was experiencing an extraordinary journey.

It began in a kind of underworld he calls the "Realm of the Earthworm's-Eye View." It's a nightmare kingdom of muck, full of artery-like roots and animal faces, vividly described in his memoir. After a long time, he glimpses an opening, and with it a guide appears:

> Someone was next to me: a beautiful girl with high cheekbones and deep
> blue eyes […] . She looked at me with a look that, if you saw it for a few
> moments, would make your whole life up to that point worth living,
> no matter what had happened in it so far. It was not a romantic look.
> It was not a look of friendship. It was a look that was somehow beyond
> all these[…] beyond all the different kinds of love we have down here

80

on earth. It was something higher, holding all those other kinds of love within itself while at the same time being more genuine and pure than all of them. (Alexander, p. 40)

With her at his side, he journeys into celestial realms, where "flocks of transparent orbs […] arced across the sky." Like many of the souls in *Paradiso*, they sing, because "if the joy didn't come out of them this way then they would simply not be able to contain it." He begins, in his mind, to ask questions of these beings, and an extraordinary thing happens:

Each time I silently posed one of these questions, the answer came instantly in an explosion of light, color, love, and beauty that blew through me like a crashing wave. What was important about these bursts was that they didn't simply silence my questions by overwhelming then. They *answered* them, but in a way that bypassed language. Thoughts entered me directly. But it wasn't thought like we experience on earth. […] These thoughts were solid and immediate—hotter than fire and wetter than water—and as I received them I was able to instantly and effortlessly understand concepts that would have taken me years to fully grasp in my earth life. (Alexander, pp. 45–6)

He experiences, in short, exactly the kind of telepathy Dante encounters in the Heaven of Venus. Finally, he approaches a dark but radiant "Core," which he sometimes calls "Om," sometimes "God." His guide has vanished by this point, as Beatrice does in the *Paradiso*. He has a similar unspoken dialogue with this "Core," in which he receives answers to many current scientific mysteries—dark energy, dark matter, multiple universes. (Similarly, Dante, as we have seen, in the terms of the philosophy of his own time, gazing into the Godhead, understands "substances, accidents, and their relations," "the universal/ form" of the "knot" of the cosmos.)

Returning to earth, Dr. Alexander retains a partial memory of these answers. But, he says, it would take years for his physical brain to recreate them, and, in any case, trying to put it into language would be "like trying to write a novel with only half the alphabet."

Dante, too, protests the inadequacy of language to convey his Beatific Vision, and even of memory to recall it:

After that, what I saw was greater than
    speech can portray, for at such a vision
    it fails, and at that extreme, memory fails.

(Paradiso XXXIII, ll. 55–7)

Or, as he puts it earlier:

    approaching near to its desire,
Our intellect sinks so deep within itself
That memory has no way to follow there.

(Paradiso I, ll. 6–9)

Dr. Alexander continued to believe in the reality of his experience, and in the inevitable inference, given the inactivity of his neocortex: that consciousness has a locus somewhere beyond the physical chemistry of the brain. This implies, for him, a self that must survive the death of the physical body. He also credits his journey for his recovery from meningitis without brain damage, for which his doctors could offer no medical explanation.

I don't know if Dr. Alexander ever read Dante. But in a way, it doesn't matter. As he discovered later, looking at a photograph, his Beatrice had the same features as a biological sister he had never met, who had died some years before. So much for literary influence. Rather an extraordinary serendipity, the human mind, at seven hundred years' distance, producing essentially the same account of our ultimate journey. In both, we find the ascent from a realm of darkness; the singing orbs; the beloved guide; the communication beyond language, which includes communication of the "universal form" of the cosmos, in the terms of the science of their respective eras. Surely these extraordinary correspondences tell us something about the deepest levels of the human mind, whether we understand them in Jungian or ontological, even religious terms.

I must remain somewhat agnostic, as most of my readers will, about the metaphysical status of Dr. Alexander's experience. But it gives me hope—not necessarily of immortality as my individual self, but that I might, like Dante, understand "in a flash" the relation, even the identity, between my peculiar human nature and the nature of the cosmos itself.

WORKS CITED

Alexander, Eben, *Proof of Heaven*, New York: Simon and Schuster, 2012.

Alighieri, Dante, *Inferno*, tr. Robert Pinsky, New York: Farrar, Straus, Giroux, 1994.

Alighieri, Dante, *Paradiso*, my own unpublished translation.

Alighieri, Dante, *Paradiso*, tr. John Sinclair, Oxford: Oxford University Press, 1961 [cited as Sinclair].

Alighieri, Dante, "Paradiso XXXIII," tr. W. S. Merwin, *Atlantic Monthly*, December 2001.

Alighieri, Dante, *Purgatorio*, tr. W. S. Merwin, New York: Alfred A. Knopf, 2000.

Alighieri, Dante, *Vita Nuova and Canzoniere*, London: J. M. Dent, 1929.

Benjamin, Jessica, *The Bonds of Love*, New York: Pantheon Books, 1988.

Bly, Robert, *Iron John*, New York: Vintage Books, 1992.

Bonaventura, Saint, *The Mind's Road to God*, tr. George Boas, Indianapolis: Bobbs-Merrill, 1953.

Campbell, Joseph, *The Hero with a Thousand Faces*, Novato: New World Library, 2008.

De Sanctis, Francesco, *De Sanctis on Dante*, tr. Joseph Rossi and Alfred Galpin, Madison: University of Wisconsin Press, 1957.

Eliot, T. S., *Dante*, London: Faber & Faber, 1929.

Jung, C. G., *Aion*, Princeton: Bollingen Series, 1959.

Jung, C. G., "Archetypes of the Collective Unconscious," *The Basic Writings of C. G. Jung*, ed. de Laszlo, New York: Random House, 1959.

Kierkegaard, Soren, *Either/Or Part II*, tr. Howard V. Hong and Edna H. Hong, Princeton: Princeton University Press, 1987.

Klein, Melanie, "A Study of Envy and Gratitude," *The Selected Melanie Klein*, ed. Juliet Mitchell, New York: The Free Press, 1986.

Lowell, Robert, *Collected Prose*, New York: Farrar, Straus, Giroux, 1987.

Works Cited

Mazur, Michael, and Robert Pinsky, *Image and Text*, Occasional Papers of the Doreen B. Townsend Center, 1994.

Merrill, James, *The Changing Light at Sandover*, New York: Alfred A. Knopf, 1992.

Montale, Eugenio, *Collected Poems*, tr. William Arrowsmith, New York: W. W. Norton, 2012.

Nemerov, Howard, "The Dream of Dante," *The Poets' Dante*, ed. Peter S. Hawkins and Rachel Jacoff, pp. 210–26, New York: Farrar, Straus, Giroux, 2001.

Pinsky, Robert, *The Figured Wheel*, New York: Farrar, Straus, Giroux, 1996.

Poggioli, Renato, "Paolo and Francesca," *Dante: A Collection of Critical Essays*, ed. John Freccero, Englewood Cliffs: Prentice Hall, 1965.

Rich, Adrienne, *Diving into the Wreck*, New York: W. W. Norton, 1973.

Rilke, Rainer Maria, *Letters to a Young Poet*, tr. Stephen Mitchell, New York: Vintage, 1986.

Schildgen, Brenda Deen, "Dante's Neologisms in the *Paradiso* and the Latin Rhetorical Tradition," *Dante Studies*, CVII (1989).

Scott, Peter Dale, *Minding the Darkness*, New York: New Directions, 2000.

Shelley, Percy Bysshe, "Epipsychidion," *Selected Poetry and Prose*, ed. Carlos Baker, New York: Random House, 1951.

Tate, Allen, "The Symbolic Imagination," *The Man of Letters in the Modern World*, New York: Meridian Books, 1955.

Winnicott, D. W., *Playing and Reality*, London and New York: Routledge, 1989.

Yeats, William Butler, *Collected Poems*, New York: MacMillan, 1964.

INDEX